THE HBCU EXPERIENCE

THE HBCU ROYAL UNIVERSITY QUEENS EDITION

Visionary Author Ashley Little

Lead Author Bridgett Herring Williams

Foreword Author Dr. Judy Rashid

Foreword Author Dale Williams

Book Cover Design: The Harbor Institute

Published By: The HBCU Experience Movement, LLC

The HBCU Experience Movement, LLC

thehbcuexperiencemovement@gmail.com

Ordering Information:

Quantity Sales: Special discounts are available on quantity purchases by corporations, associations, and nonprofits. For details, contact the publisher at the address above.

ISBN: 978-1-7349311-2-9

A Message from the Founders

Ashley Little, Fred Whit & Uche Byrd

Historically Black Colleges & Universities (HBCUs) were established to serve the educational needs of black Americans. During the time of their establishment, and many years afterward, blacks were generally denied admission to traditionally white institutions. Prior to The Civil War, there was no structured higher education system for black students. Public policy, and certain statutory provisions, prohibited the education of blacks in various parts of the nation. Today, HBCUs represent a vital component of American higher education.

The HBCU Experience Movement, LLC is a collection of stories from prominent alumni throughout the world, who share how their HBCU experience molded them into the people they are today. We are also investing financially into HBCUs throughout the country. Our goal is to create a global movement of prominent HBCU alumni throughout the nation to continue to share their stories each year, allowing us to give back to prestigious HBCUs annually.

We are proud to present to you *The HBCU Experience: The HBCU Royal University Queens Edition.* We would like to acknowledge and give a special thanks to our amazing lead author/partner, Bridgett Herring Williams, for your dedication and commitment. We appreciate you and thank you for your hard work and dedication on behalf of this project. We would also like to give a special thanks to our foreword authors, contributing authors and partners for believing in this movement and investing your time, and monetary donations, to give back to your school. We appreciate all of the The HBCU Royal University Queens who shared your HBCU experience in the FIRST EVER HBCU Queens publication.

ASHLEY LITTLE

About Ashley Little

Ashley Little is The CEO/Founder of Ashley Little Enterprises, LLC which encompasses her Media, Consulting Work, Writing, Ghost Writing, Book Publishing, Book Coaching, Project Management, Public Relations & Marketing, and Empowerment Speaking. In addition, she is an Award-Winning Serial Entrepreneur, TV/Radio Host, Speaker, Host, Philanthropist, Business Coach, Investor and 7X Best Selling Author.

She is a proud member of Delta Sigma Theta Sorority Incorporated, and a member of Alpha Phi Omega. She is very involved in her community, organizations and non-profits. Currently, she is the Co-Founder of Sweetheart Scholars Non-profit Organization 501 (C-3) along with three other powerful women. This scholarship is given out annually to African American Females from her hometown of Wadesboro, North Carolina who are attending college to help with their expenses. Ms. Little believes it takes a village to raise a child and to never forget where you come from. Ms. Little is a strong believer in giving back to her community. She believes our young ladies need vision, direction, and strong mentorship. She is the Head of the Scholarship Committee for Swing Into Their Dreams Foundation the mission of Swing Into Their Dream Foundation is E.P.I.C. Empowerment and Philanthropy In The Community. Ms. Little is also the Editor and Chief of Creating Your Seat At The Table Magazine.

She is the Founder and Owner of T.A.L.K Radio & TV Network, LLC. Airs in over 167 countries, streamed LIVE on Facebook, YouTube, Twitter and Periscope. Broadcasting and Media Production Company. This live entertainment platform is for new or existing radio shows, television shows, or other electronic media outlets, to air content from a centralized source. All news, information or music shared on this platform are solely the responsibility of the station/radio owner. She is also the Owner and Creator of Creative Broadcasting Radio Station the station of "unlimited possibilities" and Podcast, Radio/TV Host. She is also one of the hosts of the new TV Show Daytime Drama National Syndicated Television Show which will be aired on Comcast Channel 19 and ATT Channel 99 in 19 Middle Tennessee Counties. It will also air on The United Broadcasting

Network, The Damascus Roads Broadcasting Network, and Roku. She is CEO/Co-Founder of The HBCU Experience Movement LLC and CEO/Founder of Little Publishing LLC.

Ms. Little is a 5X Best Selling Author of "Dear Fear, Volume 2 18 Powerful Lessons Of Living Your Best Life Outside Of Fear", "The Gyrlfriend Code Volume 1", "I Survived", "Girl Get Up, and Win", "Glambitious Guide to Being An Entrepreneur", The Making Of A Successful Business Woman, and "Hello Queen". She is a Co-Host for The Tamie Collins Markee Radio Show, Award-Winning Entrepreneur, Reflection Contributor for the book "NC Girls Living In A Maryland World, Sales/Marketing/Contributing Writer/Event Correspondent for SwagHer Magazine, Contributing Writer for MizCEO Magazine, Contributing Editor for SheIs Magazine, ContributingWriter/National Sales Executive for Courageous Woman Magazine, Contributing Writer for Upwords International Magazine (India), Contributing Writer/Global Partner for Powerhouse Global International Magazine(London), Host of "Creating Your Seat At The Table", Host of "Authors On The Rise", Co-Host Glambitious Podcast, Partner/Visionary Author of The Gyrlfriend Code The Sorority Edition along with The Gyrlfriend Collective, LLC and Lead Author of The HBCU Experience The North Carolina A&T State University Edition. She has been on many different Podcasts, TV Shows, Magazines, and Radio Shows. Lastly, she has received awards such as "Author Of The Month", The Executive Citation of Anne Arundel County, Maryland Award which was awarded by the County Executive Steuart L. Pittman, Top 28 Influential Business Pioneers for K.I.S.H Magazine Spring 2019 Edition. She has been featured in SwagHer Magazine, Power20Magazine Glambitious, Sheen Magazine, All About Inspire Magazine, Formidable Magazine, BRAG Magazine, Sheen Magazine, Front Cover of MizCEO Magazine November 2019, Front Cover for UpWords Magazine October 2019 Edition, Courageous Woman Magazine, Courageous Woman Special Speakers Edition November 2019, Influence Magazine, Featured/Interviewed On a National Syndicated Television Show HBCU 101 on Aspire TV, Dynasty of Dreamers K.I.S.H Magazine Spring 2019 Edition, Dynasty of Dreamers K.I.S.H Magazine September 2019 Edition, Front Cover of Courageous Magazine December 2019, Front

Cover of Doz International Magazine January 2020, Top 28 Influential Business Pioneers for K.I.S.H Magazine, Power20 Magazine Glambitious January 2020, Power20 Magazine Glambitious February 2020, Featured in Powerhouse Global International London Magazine March 2020 edition, Featured in Sheen Magazine February 2020 as one of "The Top 20 Women To Be On The Lookout For In 2020, Awarded National Women's Empowerment Ministry "Young, Gifted, & Black Award" February 2020 which honors and celebrate women in business such as Senior Level Executives, Entrepreneurs and CEO's below age 40 for their creativity and business development. Featured in National Women Empowerment Magazine 2020 as well to name a few.

Ms. Little received her undergraduate degree in English from North Carolina A&T State University. Next, she received her Master's Degree in Industrial Organizational Psychology. Ms. Little is a mover and shaker and she continuously pushes herself to be better than she was yesterday. She gives GOD all the credit for everything that has happened in her life. She has strong faith and determination to be great. She believes her only competition is herself. Her favorite scripture is Philippians 4:13 "I can do all things through Christ who strengthens me".

UCHE BYRD

About Uche Byrd

Uche Byrd was born and raised on the Southside of Chicago. As a graduate from The North Carolina Agricultural and Technical State University, Uche not only obtained his Bachelor's degree in Applied Mathematics, but he also went on to earn a Master's degree in Industrial Engineering. During his tenure at the HBCU, Uche was fortunate enough to pledge the Mu Psi Chapter of Omega Psi Phi Fraternity, Inc., as well as to hold the position of Mr. Aggie. Uche also served as the Region 2 Pre-College Initiative Chair for the National Society of Black Engineers and Vice President of the Midwest Aggie Club. As a Resident Assistant at The Aggie Suites, Uche was a mentor and motivation to many. Today, Uche resides in northeast Washington, D.C. with his wife and son, and serves as the Metro Area Youth Federation Leader for the Allegheny East Conference of the Seventh-Day Adventist Church, where he works with the youth programing for 30+ churches in the D.C., Maryland and Virginia areas.

FRED WHITAKER

About Fred Whitaker

When passion, performance and perseverance come together, a force to be reckoned with is created. Frederick Whitaker, known industry-wide as Fred Whit, has become a well-known name due to his business strategies and negotiative saavy, behind the scenes of the entertainment industry. He is a believer in the mantra hard work pays off, and has lived this mantra everyday of his professional life.

These days, stars such as actor and media personalities Terrence J and La La Anthony, filmmaker Will Packer, and a host of others, call on him when they need unique jobs done in a professional and dignified manner. He rises to any occasion and consistently exceeds expectations.

Growing up between the make or break city of New York and resolute small towns of rural North Carolina, Fred developed his acumen as a polished businessman. New York introduced Fred to the meaning of "hustle" and "ambition" with North Carolina yielding a certain Southern compassion and charm. Now the man the industry sees has the experience and ability to single-handedly take numerous careers to the next level.

As manager of Terrence J (*E! News,Think Like A Man1& 2*) he secures major roles and television deals and brand integration for the rising star. Fred was instrumental in Terrence landing exclusive endorsements with Crown Royal and Jeep. In addition, Fred successfully planned the rollout for La La Anthony's *New York Times*best seller book, *The Love Playbook: Rules for Love, Sex, and Happiness*. Furthermore, Fred consults for radio host Angela Yee NYC's Power 105 morning show) with more deals in the works. Wearing many hats, he never loses sight of his main goal – to provide incomparable service for each of his clients. Fred proves, as his company motto states, it is the little things you do in life that make all the difference.

Fred has always had a knack for making something out of nothing. While in college at NC A&T State University, he coordinated various large campus events. After graduating with a degree in communications, Fred took steps on a path he didn't imagine himself traveling. "I had no experience in management, so everything I have accomplished over the last fifteen years, I learned on the job," he states. One many occasions he's played the role of assistant, manager, accountant, provided service to whatever was needed for completion. As is this isn't enough, Fred has also negotiated several deals with McDonald's, Sean John, and Samsung, as he goes on to gain favor across multiple branding platforms.

A devout humanitarian, he makes time to organize charity events, toy drives, raising funds and giving away almost $10,000 worth of clothes to the Salvation Army, annually. Fred finds it difficult to build his empire without breathing life into the progress of others.

Success is measured by loving what you do, and making things happen while doing it. As doors continue to open, Fred will never forget those moments where his destiny was uncertain, but he believed his dreams of success would certainly come true. Those dreams have not only come into fruition, they are growing far beyond his imagination. An admirable being and determined man, Fred Whitaker has become a staple in the industry, all while shaping the lives of not only those who achieve fame, but everyday people as well.

TABLE OF CONTENTS

DR. JUDY NAZIRAH RASHID

Foreword

Dr. Judy Nazirah Rashid

Advisor to Miss A&T 1990-2010

On November 30, 1974 there appeared a strange fossil, which was determined to be three and half million years old, in the Olduvai Gorge in Northern , Tanzania. Olduvai Gorge is a site that holds the earliest evidence of the existence of human ancestors. Paleoanthropologists have found hundreds of fossilized bones and stone tools in the area dating back millions of years, leading them to conclude that humans evolved in Africa. (https://www.livescience.com/40455-olduvai-gorge.html) The fossil , found by paleontologists, was the remains of an African woman whom they affectionately named LUCY. History has since recorded , and as cited by Simone Schwarz –Bart in her book In Praise of Black Women-Ancient African Queens , that *Lucy is the grandmother to us all, blacks and whites, yellows, reds, people of the sea and dwellers of the steppe, those who live with the sun or with the polar cold.* She is undisputed as the one womb from which all of humanity came.

Help me salute Mother Queen *Lucy*, also known as Black Eve, and all of her daughters , the Queens of Historically Black Colleges and Universities of the 20th and 21st century. They honor those who came before them and lead generations forward. They are poised, spiritual, intelligent, caring, and beautiful. They are courageous, and daring as they lead. They are honorable yet wear their titles humbly for life as they serve the people who made them queen. They are the voice for the voiceless and have hope for the hopeless. They are the sum total of womanhood at its finest. Once a queen, always a queen. Listen to their stories; be inspired to serve.

Written by Dr. Judy Rashid

University Queen Advisor, 1991-2011

About Dr. Judy Nazirah Rashid

Dr. Judy Nazirah Rashid is Founder and CEO of Skills Training and Development Consulting Services (STADCS). She has been involved in education for the last 44 years as teacher and school principal (K-12), senior student affairs administrator, and as adjunct faculty in Liberal Studies (Conflict Resolution) and the PhD Program in Leadership Studies. As the Associate Vice Chancellor for Student Affairs, she supervised Student Conduct, International Students, Veterans and Student Disability Support Services, Multicultural Students, Greek Life, and Student Government where she also supervised the University Queens for 20 years.

She recently retired as the Associate Vice Chancellor for Student Affairs / Dean of Students from her undergraduate alma mater, North Carolina A&T State University. Currently she serves as an Adjunct Assistant Professor in the Dept. of Adult Education and Leadership Studies.

Since 1989, Dr. Rashid has been professionally involved in conflict management education and training including international conflict resolution in South Africa. For almost two decades , she has garnered financial educational support for South African youth and adults. In December 2019, a recently erected building in Vanderjilpark , South Africa was name the Dr. Judy Rashid Education and Leadership Center.

Dr. Rashid received her Bachelor of Science and Masters' degrees (both summa cum laude) from North Carolina A&T and her doctoral degree in higher education administration from North Carolina State University in Raleigh. She holds certification in both interaction management and performance management from the State of North Carolina, advanced training in teaching negotiation in the organization from Harvard University, complete course training in N.C. Law for Non-Attorney Mediators, Mediation Certification Training/N.C. Superior Court Mediated Settlement Conferences, and Mediation Certification Training/Equal Employment Opportunity Commission.

Dr. Rashid is a member of the N.C. Bar Association (Dispute Resolution Section) and the NC Association of Retired Governmental Employees. Dr. Rashid dedicates her civic life through service to the less fortunate and is a Charter Member of both the National Museum of African American History and Culture of Washington D.C. and of the International African American Museum in Charleston, S.C.

Dr. Rashid is married and has two adult sons and an outstanding grandson.

DALE MICHELLE WILLIAMS

Foreword

Dale Michelle Williams

Miss Tennessee State University 1992-1993

The idea of being a college queen for many young women seems like a dream come true, but for many of the writers in this book it has been a life-changing reality that has shaped them into the women they are today. Nothing is more exhilarating than for a young African American female to be honored by her peers and University for her ability to lead as an official student spokesperson. Upon winning, she becomes a part of history that is embedded in African American tradition forever.

Being an HBCU college queen is a time-honored tradition I will never forget. Through years of research, I have learned that these positions are uniquely different from any other "Miss" title in existence. As you read these personal accounts in this book, you will get an inside look at life changing moments when some African American women have gained acceptance, love, and confidence, while others experienced growth, learned lessons, and received opportunities, but with each reign, a queen emerged. Not the queen that comes because you won the title, but the queen that connects you to something bigger than yourself. It is at this point that one realizes just how these positions evolve and speak to the pride and tradition of HBCU colleges and universities, thus highlighting their mission to develop not just the mind but the whole person. These colleges and universities saw fit to place honor on African American women not only for their beauty, but also for their academic accomplishments and leadership skills. Yet accomplishments and leadership have never been an issue for African American women, as we have excelled in so many areas. Still, many will say they struggle to see themselves as beautiful.

Our young women need to understand that they are beautiful though the world counters our beauty and sublimely chips away at our self-esteem. Who can forget the 2011 *Psychology Today* article by psychologist Satoshi Kanazawa titled "Why Are Black Women Less Physically Attractive Than

Other Women?" Although the article was met with outrage, the reality is black women are the least represented in our versatility in a beautiful way. Thus, when I became a black college queen for the first time, I felt represented. HBCUs created the position of campus queen to uplift black women because the world sometimes placed us under its feet. However, on HBCU campuses, the queen is special and honored by her community. HBCU queens can be traced to the 1920s when these college and universities found themselves emphasizing new images of black people, and black women were no exception. The creation of the HBCU queen gave African Americans the ability to create their own image of beauty. By the 1970s, thanks to *Ebony* magazine's annual spotlight of campus queens, just about every HBCU college and university had an African-American female to represent their campus. Today HBCU queens serve their institutions in various ways as spokespersons, recruiters, and leaders. Many serve as a beacon of hope to young impressionable minds wanting to go to college, as well as role models, mentors, and leaders to their peers. Each queen can attest to witnessing the glimmer in a little girl's eye when she has encountered the presence of an HBCU queen because we know for the first time, she sees herself.

While each HBCU campus has created their own model and standard of what it means to be "queen," we can all agree that she will always be a part of African American history and culture. I am not aware of any other program that has fully represented the African American female as a whole, focusing on our best attributes externally and internally. Consequently, we must never forget the HBCU queen and the contributions she has made, what she represents, or negate her experiences. Her unique historical position is just as important now as it was then. In a world that devalues black women and coins us at times in the most negative ways, these leadership positions remind young women of the importance of their worth. HBCUs saw the queen in us, and for that we will be forever grateful. This is our story. This is the *HBCU Royal University Queens Edition*.

To Be a Queen

You know I try to make people understand
It's not the way I wave my hand
It's not the things I do or say
It's not my walk, lean or sway
It's just the little things in me
that let me know that
I'm a queen
To be a queen
I am a queen
In my heart.
It's not the crown that I wore
Or the title that I bore
It's just what I choose to do
Because of my love for my HBCU
To be a queen
I am their queen
In my heart.

- *Dale-licately said*

Dale Williams is the founder of Leadership for Queens, host of HBCU Kings and Queens Conference, and served as Miss Tennessee State University 1992-1993.

About Dale Michelle Williams

Dale Williams is the founder of Leadership for Queens, a leadership conference for Historically Black University and College (HBCU) Queens. She has organized and conducted the conference annually for HBCU queens and kings for 19 years. She has more than 20 years of experience in higher education. Currently, Dale is an academic advisor at University of Memphis as well as an instructor at Bethel University. She is a sought after trainer and speaker that has also worked at many HBCU's in a variety of capacities. Dale's leadership aspirations began early as she was not only queen of her high school (Hamilton) in Memphis, TN, but also Miss Tennessee State University (TSU) 1992-93. Dale has judged and worked with various pageants, served as a motivational keynote speaker and conducted numerous leadership workshops at various universities, conferences and community events. She believes that those who walk in such positions as the HBCU king or queen have the perfect opportunity to make a great impact on others. Dale is a member of community/public service organizations such as Delta Sigma Theta Sorority, Inc., Junior League of Memphis and TSU Alumni Association. She received a Bachelor of Science degree in Speech Communications and Theatre and a Master's of Arts in English from Tennessee State University. She has a graduate certificate in African-American Literature from University of Memphis. She thoroughly enjoys helping young men and women reach their goals and realize their full potential. She enjoys giving back to her community.

http://hbcukingsandqueens.com/
https://twitter.com/HBCUKNQ
https://www.instagram.com/hbcukingsandqueens/
https://www.facebook.com/HBCUKingsandQueens/
https://www.facebook.com/ms.williams.35
https://www.facebook.com/dale.michelle.3
https://www.youtube.com/watch?v=5Kb7tnzLXuY&feature=youtu.be
Official Hashtag
#LQKK

BRIDGETT HERRING WILLIAMS

The Bracelet

Bridgett Herring Williams

Miss North Carolina A&T State University 1997-1998

I couldn't stop crying. Lying hopelessly defeated in the fetal position on the office floor of my advisor, I was...*crying*...*hysterically crying*. In this moment, I was inconsolable. This was so far from the composure of my character. Still, this time, I couldn't hold back the dam of tears that poured relentlessly down my face and neck as each breath flooded my heart with overwhelming anxiety. I was in disbelief. This simply could not be happening. This couldn't be true. I'd worked meticulously every day for months. Now, this! I didn't want to disappoint anyone. I had so much riding on this. Everything had to be perfect. *I* had to be perfect because, after all, all eyes would be on me, the *queen*.

I was *Miss A&T* 1997-1998.

I will never forget the day I was crowned Miss A&T. It was October 30, 1997. Although I was crowned at a coronation ceremony later that evening, I had already *become* Miss A&T. My ascension began after a breakdown. A breakdown that landed me on the floor, sobbing in front of my advisor, whom I always went to when I needed sound advice and had challenges. Upon composing myself, I explained my uncommon hysteria to her. I explained that the purchase order for the bracelets I wanted for my court and myself had not been submitted. After staying up all night to make sure Corbett Sports Center was going to look perfect for the queen's coronation that evening, all the rehearsals, the dress fittings, and no drama between the young ladies on my court, we were not going to have bracelets.

This was not happening. The perfect day, the day I had worked all summer to plan, was going to be ruined over *bracelets*. I know you read "bracelets" and you may be asking, "Are you serious? You were on the floor hyperventilating over some jewelry?" To that I say, "Yes," but "No." It wasn't about the bracelets from a material sense, but rather what the bracelets represented. They represented *respect.*

It was my junior year, and I had a strong desire to create a mentoring program for the girls at a local middle school in Greensboro, North Carolina. There was already a program for the boys in place; however, nothing had been established for the girls. My desire was to create a mentoring relationship that would allow young black girls to see and connect with positive, ambitious examples of themselves in everyday society. I wanted to do that through counsel and interaction with my peers and myself. I have a passion for serving young people, especially young ladies. That is what was taught to me. It is the legacy of mentorship and counsel that I learned from the matriarchs in my life, including my mother, Mariam; my grandmothers, Alice and Ruth; my aunts, Portia and Patricia; and my Godmother, Della. Making them proud meant that I should be authentically me, understanding that being a queen is not a one-size-fits-all crown.

I was the heir to the throne. I was the legacy of all my sister queens. But before them, I was the legacy of the queens who raised me. They taught me the "black girl magic" of being in the front and the back at the same time; that is, leading from the frontline while providing encouragement and support from the back. A queen embraces all that she is and she does not conform to what others may project upon her. She listens to wise counsel around her and humbly accepts advice. A queen looks out for others with an open heart while challenging herself, and those around her, to produce the best version of themselves.

I was taught a culture of sisterhood, strength and self-pride. I wanted to share this mantra in my new mentoring program, Aggie Q.U.E.E.N.S. These young ladies would exhibit Quality, Understanding and Enrichment through Education, Nurturing and Success. This was the motivating factor in me deciding to run for Miss A&T. The respect associated with the position would turn up the volume of my voice and help influence greater change. Therefore, it became my mission to operate in excellence and to operate in perfection—as a leader, as a professional and as a young black woman. I wanted to leave no room for doubt so there was absolutely no room for error. Perfection equated to control and control garnered respect.

So regarding the bracelet, it was never about the jewelry. It was about the perfect presentation of an expectation. An expectation--one I created for myself where I had to be the perfect representative of my peers. I arrived at meetings and events on time, wearing all the right things, saying all the right things, and making all the right community connections to push my platform forward as a responsible student. Yet and still, on this day, in that moment, I realized that no matter how hard I tried, I would never be *perfect*. I had to break out of those narrow expectations. That need to be perfect. By default, that had me feeling like a failure. I felt like a failure for not meeting expectations, which was also my biggest fear.

Ironically, on the day that I was to be crowned Miss A&T, I was still being mentored by my advisor, just as much as the middle school girls I had come to mentor. My advisor listened to me with a calm ear. She encouraged me and helped me resolve the issue by contacting a former queen, who stepped in to provide the bracelets. The network of sisterhood and support that I have received from my experiences as an HBCU Queen has been an invaluable tool and asset in my journey and approach to mentoring. Being able to innerstand and identify with girls of our culture allows me to relate just how we all have our own bracelet story.

Your bracelets, unlike mine, may not have been living up to a certain expectation. Your bracelet may be colorism, anxiety, feelings of inadequacy, bravery, financial issues, educational challenges and more. The list goes on and on for the personal challenges one may face. As a black person, it is evident that we all feel we have to work harder or prove ourselves just for status quo. But there is also the game *within the game* that *black women* encounter. You have to work even harder to prove that you're smarter than the intellect of men's pride. You know the feeling that you must be Superwoman to everyone around you. For me, on that particular day, it was a minor expectation that I assigned a major role to. It was a box of perfection, an image that I had to maintain for respect. After all, part of knowing the role is looking the part. Right?

I guess it all depends on the character you play. Are you playing a role true to the audience in your life, or is it true to the audience within yourself? I can answer for me. Attending an HBCU taught me that I do not have to play a character. Too often this is the stigma perpetuated and placed on African-Americans, especially black women. We must fit into a mold or box to keep the peace and not incite insecurity within the system of patriarchal pride. No. This is not my truth. I simply have to educate myself about myself and be what I am--*Queen.* And, as a queen representing an HBCU, you understand that queens are diverse. They have different hair. Some wear makeup while others wear no makeup. They have different beliefs and they come in different shades. I learned that being a true queen is not about your title. Instead, it's about your nature. A crown does not dictate a queen. It's not about the jewels that you put on to adorn yourself. Instead, it's about the jewels you develop within.

Attending an HBCU has the great benefit of allowing one to discover themselves in a familiar community, while also establishing and building pride in a culturally safe environment. During that year, I learned to intertwine my greatness with the haunting of my flaws. That one year inevitably changed my life forever. My HBCU was undoubtedly important to me, and to represent her was one of the greatest honors I have ever had. Being Miss A&T taught me so much about myself. I am still a *queen.*

It took me a long time to accept myself for who I am, for my flaws and successes. I have discovered and nurtured the woman within me. My passion continues to evolve with my growth, and I continue to uplift our young black women in today's atmosphere of individuality and acceptance. I am more than any bracelet I could ever wear. The true beauty of a queen is her character. The value within that cannot be contained. You've heard it before. Tiara: $450. Gown and shoes: $2,500. Jewelry: $250. Heart of a Queen – *Priceless.*

I hope you enjoy the stories of joy and triumph each of my Sister Queens share.

Lead Author Bridgett Herring Williams

About Bridgett Herring Williams

Bridgett Herring Williams received her undergraduate degree in Construction Management from North Carolina A&T State University and a Master's in Public Administration from High Point University.

While a student at A&T, Bridgett was an active student leader, serving in many capacities and represented her alma mater as Miss North Carolina A&T State University, 1997-98. Upon graduation from college, Bridgett began a career in construction as an assistant project manager while also pursuing her passion for inner city youth, by volunteering for the local Boys and Girls Club. Thru her volunteerism, Bridgett learned more about the non-profit sector which eventually led to her career change. Dedicating almost 20 years to the non-profit sector, Bridgett has vast experiences as a program director to an executive director. Her demonstrated expertise has been in program development, grant writing, facilitating partnerships, consulting, and leading fundraising campaigns for non-profits of various sizes and missions. Working with the Boys & Girls Clubs of America, YMCA, Boy Scouts of America and the Marilyn G. Rabb Foundation, Bridgett learned the challenges of non-profit leadership from many different points of view. Additionally, she facilitates leadership development and management seminars and workshops for other community and faith based organizations. Having returned to her roots, Bridgett is currently the Director of Development for the College of Science & Technology at A&T and the Vice President of Albri Logistics, a transportation business she co-owns with her husband.

Bridgett is certain her primary purpose in life is to serve young people, most especially young women. She has served on several boards and held committee leadership positions within community organizations including Friends of Macedonia, JAL3 Ministries, Goodwill Industries, Project Potential, Cabarrus Charter Academy, Next Generation-The Movement, Charlotte-Mecklenburg Schools, Homeless Shelter Network and Keep Mecklenburg Beautiful. Her volunteer service has also expanded internationally with Samaritan's Feet in White River, South Africa.

She is a member of Delta Sigma Theta Sorority, Inc., National Council for Negro Women, the National Association of Women Professionals, Queen City Alumni Chapter of North Carolina A&T State University, the advisory board of 1,2,3 JUMP and serves as a consultant for several brands in the fashion and entertainment industry as well as non-profit organizations. Bridgett is a contributing author in 'The HBCU Experience Anthology-The North Carolina A&T State University Edition'.

Though her life serving the community is fulfilling, her greatest joy comes in spending time with her husband and daughter.

SHAKARA L. PARKS

The Measure of a True Queen

Shakara L. Parks

Miss Morris College 2009-2010

The year 2005 was the year I thought I would never compete for a title ever again after losing in the Miss Timberland Pageant, my high school alma mater. Now that I think back to that night, I felt extremely low—not because I did not win—but because of all the hard work I put in. It was only five of us who competed, and I did not get anything. Not even a certificate of appreciation.

"What's next, Shakara? You are a natural born leader and a queen! Do not give up!"

Those were the words my mom told me on our way home after the pageant and coronation. It stuck with me until I got to college. During my freshman year at Morris College, my group leader, former queen, Iashea Simmons, was the reigning Miss Morris College. She was a person (and still is) who would build you back up and pour energy into you. If it were not for her, and the example she set, I would have never had the courage to compete for another title and run for Miss Morris College.

In April of 2009, flyers advertising the upcoming Miss Morris competition went up around campus. I instantly called my mom to ask if I should compete in the pageant. Of course, she told me, "Yes!" Before I knew it, my family came together to help with my campaign. After two weeks of campaigning, "It's Time For Nunu," which included hanging posters, spirit-driven activities, a specialized mixtape by a local DJ with an intro like no other, and a speech before the entire student body, the moment I had been anticipating and waiting for had finally arrived. I, Ms. Shakara Theirse, was crowned the 2009-2010 Miss Morris College.

While reigning as Miss Morris, I learned to treat myself like the queen my mom always told me I was. Being a queen allowed me to love myself more with much more confidence. This moment in my life made me feel like more than a just a queen. It made me feel like a woman who did not allow a past loss to dictate her future and purpose. After my coronation, "A Night of Enchantment and Divine Inspirations," a fire reignited inside of me. My goal then became to use my life and my experiences as an example for others. I always knew deep down inside that I wanted to pour into the lives of young girls in such a way that others, such as Iashea, had poured into me. One such opportunity for me to use my life as a class came four years later when I was hired to choreograph the very pageant that I lost at my high school alma mater, Timberland High School. At first, I wondered if it would be a good idea to choreograph the pageant. I thought, *What would people think of me since I lost and now would be choreographing?* Thankfully, I stopped listening to that voice in my head and put all those self-doubting thoughts aside. I allowed God's voice to lead me.

True to His Word, God turned my so-called failure into endless opportunities. Not only did I choreograph the Miss Timberland pageant, but I became a choreographer and pageant coach for local K-12 schools, Miss Black & Gold pageants, Delta Sigma Theta, Inc. Cotillions, Miss Morris College coronations, and much more. My career as a choreographer took off. I always look back on my high school defeat and future win as Miss Morris as the two major impacts in my life. Had I never experienced what I thought was a devasting loss, I would have never tapped into the destiny God had for my life. None of my experiences thus far have been a waste. Being a queen has molded me into the business owner, pageant coach and mentor I am today.

I want to leave this with anyone who ever thought about giving up after a loss: Sometimes, our lives are set up like a GPS. We set our destination to the place we would like to go, but what we do not realize is that there may be roadblocks, red lights, stop signs and alternate routes we did not anticipate on the journey ahead. No matter what it looks like, we must continue to follow our life map and listen to our inner voice that says, "Take the road to success. Never give up. Make a U-turn. In 2.5 miles, continue praying. Failure up ahead! Keep watch of life's speed bumps that might try to slow you down." Even while in traffic, you must ask God for patience—no matter how long you must sit in it.

I have not yet made it to my destination, and I've had many pitstops along the way. In 2006, I met the love of my life. In 2009, I was crowned Miss Morris College. In 2010, I graduated cum laude from the illustrious Morris College. In 2012, I opened the K. Lynese Center for the Arts. In 2014, my handsome and healthy baby boy was born. In 2015, my K. Lynese team won their very first dance competition out of 44 teams from all over the United States. In 2016, the love of my life made me his fiancée. In 2017, I survived Sepsis and married the man of my dreams. In 2018, my life slowed down.

The signs I alluded to earlier were ahead of me. I sacrificed my dream and took an unplanned, yet necessary, U-turn. My sweet and supportive mother became ill, and I, being the oldest of my siblings, immediately acted and became her caregiver. It was time to be there for the woman who was my first coach, the woman who had always been there for me. My role as my mother's caregiver led to me closing my dance studio and quitting a career I always wanted as a news producer. From February 18, 2018 to November 6, 2018, I reflected on the words my mother told me after losing the Miss Timberland Pageant.

"What's next, Shakara? You are a natural born leader and a queen! Do not give up!" Now the roles were reversed.

I asked her, "What's next, Mommy? I need you. Keep fighting and do not give up." My mom fought Pulmonary Fibrosis for six years.

Her last words to me were, "Shakara, you are a strong woman. You got this!"

Those words are stamped in my personal life billboard. Any time I feel like my road is coming to an end, I replay my mom's last words. After closing the K. Lynese Center for the Arts in January of 2019, I renamed it K. Lynese Dance Company, LLC and opened three locations. In February of 2019, I had the opportunity to become the new National Director &

Choreographer for National Miss UNCF Coronation. To date, in the months of April and May, I have coached four pageant contestants and won all four titles. In June of 2019, my husband and I became homeowners. In October of 2019, I became a full-time cosmetology student, which happens to be another passion of mine.

Now the year is 2020, and the world has completely stopped due to the Coronavirus pandemic. Some may think I'm crazy, but I'm thankful for yet another pitstop in my life. During this time, God knows I was about to go full speed ahead in life's journey. There is so much I want to accomplish in life. Let's go back to February 20, 2020, a day that was full of joy and tears when my husband and I found out we were expecting. A week later, to be exact, we miscarried, and I experienced yet another loss. I honestly did not know how to feel, but then I thought, *Why not me?* Who would have thought that, after the world took a pause, my body was able to as well? There was a tremendous blessing from God! We were pregnant again 17 days after the miscarriage.

After every storm, there is truly a rainbow. I cannot wait to meet my miracle baby. On March 29, 2020, I tossed and turned. I could not sleep knowing I was beginning online classes the next morning. Who would have thought that my mother would come visit me in my dreams?

This time, she said, "Sit down, Shakara and Asa. I'm about to have your gender reveal!"

I said, "No, mom. We lost the baby."

She gave me a look as if to say, "Oh! You do not know what our God can do!" She stressed to me in the dream that I was pregnant, and she revealed that it was a girl. But it was *twins*. When I woke up, I felt so nauseous. I instantly called my husband to tell him we were pregnant.

He said, "Well, Shakara, let's get a test!" Later that evening, my life took a shift. At the time of writing this, I was eight weeks pregnant. We would not know for sure if we were having twins until June 4, 2020. My doctor told us that this was a promising pregnancy and that the baby had an extraordinarily strong heartbeat. This pandemic molded me into someone who can enjoy the little things, family times, believe in miracles, discover new passion, embrace every possibility, keep my faith and trust in God and show gratitude. I follow my heart in decision making because my life is now! I look forward to sharing my story and networking with other queens.

Remember these words: "The measure of a true queen is how many queens you have molded into the women they are today!"

About Shakara L. Parks

Shakara L. Parks is a proud native of Pineville SC; she is the mother of a handsome 5 year-old son, Ayden Jaye Parks and the wife of Asa Parks III. Shakara is one of four children of O'Toole and the Late Linnea Smalls Theirse. She attended the public schools of Berkeley County graduating from Timberland High School in 2006. She furthered her education at Morris College in Sumter, SC and was crowned Miss Morris College 2009-2010 receiving her Bachelors in Fine Arts in 2010 with Cum Laude honors. Shakara is known internationally for her triple threat abilities in dancing/choreography, singing and acting.

Because of her well-known talents and dedication, she began her career at the age of 14 as a choreographer. Today she choreograph routines for many organizations, pageants, churches, coronations, weddings, and music artist around the South Atlantic Region and Internationally. Shakara also serves her community through her sorority, Alpha Kappa Alpha Sorority INC. in which she became part of the Nu Gamma Chapter of Morris College in the Fall of 2007.

February 2017, Shakara was diagnosed with Sepsis, which is the body's overactive response to an infection in the body. More than 1 million Americans are diagnosed with this infection each year and estimated that between 28% and 50% of those diagnosed do not make it. After surviving Shakara made it her duty to bring awareness which saved a lot of lives. She stands strong with other survivors but she didn't allow Sepsis to hold her back. Shakara is now bringing awareness to the lungs disease Pulmonary Fibrosis her mother battled for 6 years.

Shakara is passionate about serving her community, mentoring young women and putting a smile on each and everyone's face that she encounters. She believes that we can all make change in this world only if we all play our part.

NICOLE WATLINGTON

Go Big!

Nicole Watlington

Miss North Carolina A&T State University 2000-2001

For so long in life, I played it safe. I accepted challenges I knew I could win. In the past, I sought challenges that did not test me. Nevertheless, making the decision to run for the title of Miss North Carolina Agricultural & Technical State University (NCA&TSU) was, up to that moment, the most frightening decision I had ever made. I considered everything that could go wrong. *What if I lose? What if no one votes for me? What if people laugh at my efforts?*

But then, something happened! I became weary of thinking about all the things that could go *wrong*. Simultaneously, I thought about all of the things that could go right.

There comes a time in life when we know it is time to mature. In order to do so, we must step outside of our comfort zones. We have been disillusioned to believe that comfort zones feel good. When we think of the word comfort, we think of things that feel good: a big cozy blanket, a romantic movie or great food. We know things we like. However, the comfort zone is synonymous with the familiar. Even if it does not feel good, it is *still* comfortable. It is comfortable because we know what to expect. Whether it be good or bad, we know what to expect.

Running for Miss NCA&TSU (more fondly referred to as Miss A&T) hurled me right out of my comfort zone. Many times, our loved ones can see our potential much sooner than we can ever conceive the idea. When I made the decision to attend this revered institution of higher education, my god sister called me Miss A&T. She talked about my campaign and how I was going to make a wonderful queen. I always smiled and laughed because I thought it was a funny joke. Who knew then that she was planting a seed? I certainly did not.

During my freshman year, I became a Golden Delight dancer in the NCA&TSU marching band, which was a huge accomplishment for me. I had never been a member of a marching band. I had been a cheerleader since middle school, and I wanted to try something different. A close friend of mine taught me how to twirl a flag (which was a required skill) and convinced me to try out. Although this role was outside of my comfort zone, it was not *too* far out of range. Besides, if I didn't make it, I had never marched before. So, I really had nothing to lose.

Becoming a member of the marching band taught me more lessons than I could have ever imagined. There were times when I wanted to quit and throw in the towel. But I had worked so hard and come so far; therefore, quitting was not an option. It was extremely trying, and it required a work ethic like none I had experienced previously. Retrospectively, some experiences in life require us to dig deep within to find personal strength and to find the will to keep going. Oftentimes, it is a prominent, singular moment when we are ready to abandon the task or goal that we are just inches away from accomplishing.

Like it was yesterday, I remember my first performance with the marching band. We were in our fitted uniforms wearing flawless makeup. We stepped proudly in shiny boots, ready to take the field. I was so nervous! While walking on the field, I reminded myself of the hard work and dedication I had put forth throughout the entire process. I thoroughly prepared for this moment. It was time to, "Give the people what they wanted."

It was an *amazing* experience! "Aggie Pride," a signature phrase voiced when referring to NCA&TSU, took on an even greater meaning. As I advanced through my college career, trying new experiences, growing academically, and giving back to the community, my love for the university increased astronomically. The spring of my sophomore year, I was ready for a new challenge. I decided to become a member of the Student Government Association. I was elected as junior class treasurer. It was working in the SGA that I also witnessed the impact of Miss A&T. I watched Gabrielle Hurtt, Miss A&T of 1999-2000. I watched how she displayed confidence, poise and determination to make a difference as a representative of the institution. I entertained the idea that maybe I could be the next Miss A&T. I remembered the seed that had been planted a few years prior. The once unimaginable was now becoming a realistic possibility. But was the possibility in my head only, or did others see it in me as well?

We were not created to experience life alone. Our support systems or chosen tribes can promote or be detrimental to our success. Hence, it is important to have positive, genuine people surrounding us. It's important to have people who love us, who will help us reach our goals, and people who will not be afraid to tell us the truth. I discussed my thoughts of running for the title with a few friends. Every single friend demonstrated support and excitement, without question. They were so anxious to support me that it almost terrified me. Doubt once again ensued as I imagined running for the title, then disappointing my family and friends if I did not win. While fear flooded me momentarily, at the same time, I also felt excited about the possibility.

My year as Miss NCA&T (2000-2001) was an awesome experience that I will forever cherish. As with any worthy process, there were peaks and valleys. Once again, I was driven out of my comfort zone. I had to reflect on my past experiences where fears and doubts attempted to hold me hostage. Nevertheless, I proudly wore the crown, represented my university, and executed programs that left a significant impact.

Since graduating from NCA&TSU, I have continued to hear doubt and feel fears. After all, I am an imperfect human being, however, I recall memories as my motivation to remind me that I have defied doubt and faced fears in the past and, whatever challenge lies ahead, I can overcome it. Today, as a school counselor and private practice mental health therapist, I am committed to empowering individuals to overcome their fears and doubts. In fact, I challenge individuals to feel their fears and go forward anyway. Besides, if our goals do not scare us or give us pause, then perhaps they are not big enough.

We often place limits on ourselves, not realizing how far we can really go. Every experience that comes our way deposits a little something in us to help conquer the next challenge. Giving in to fear could result in missing out on a moment that could change our entire lives.

Let go of where you think you should be and embrace where you are. We can save ourselves tremendous heartache when we release that image of where we think we should be. As the old hymn says, "Time is filled with swift transition." Think about how much time we have wasted licking our wounds because we are not where we think we should be. Remaining in such a place robs us of the joy of the present. The present really is a gift; however, we will not see and/or experience the value of that gift if we do not treat it as such. Make a conscious, deliberate decision today to stop living in fear. Take the risk and live your best life on purpose!

Go big!

About Nicole Watlington

Nicole Watlington served as Miss North Carolina Agricultural & Technical State University (NCA&TSU) during 2000-2001. In 2001, she earned a Bachelor of Arts degree in Psychology. During her tenure as an undergraduate, she was very active on campus. In the role of Miss NCA&T, she developed TACT (Teaching Alternatives to the Children of Tomorrow), a program for college students to mentor elementary students in the community. In addition, she led the charge for students to take a stand against domestic violence by organizing the "Take Back the Night" march across campus. Immediately after graduation, continuing her education was a goal. She completed the Master of Science degree in Adult Education in 2003 at NCA&T. She later worked in non-profit organizations in Washington, DC and Charlotte, NC. She returned to her alma mater as a professional development training specialist. In 2014, earned a Master of Science degree in Counseling. Currently, Nicole is a school counselor with the Guilford County School System. As a National Certified Counselor and Licensed Clinical Mental Health Counselor, she founded Rising Phoenix Counseling and Consulting Services in 2017. A motivational speaker who seeks to break the stigma of mental health illness in the African American community, Nicole is also committed to empowering individuals and families to overcome difficulties and to moving forward and living their best lives with purpose. Among many proud moments in her life, the most special one is being mother to two wonderful children, Aiden and Taylor.

LAKIL MASON

Limitless

Lakil Mason

Miss Morris College 2016-2017

"For me, becoming isn't about arriving somewhere or achieving a certain aim. I see it instead as forward motion, a means of evolving, a way to reach continuously toward a better self.

The journey doesn't end."

-Michelle Obama

I must admit: I knew absolutely nothing about college, including Historically Black Colleges and Universities (HBCUs). That goes for the application process, too. Embarrassing, right? My mother graduated high school as a teen mom and my father was a high school dropout who later obtained his GED. My oldest brother attended a private university on a basketball scholarship for a year before getting in trouble with the law. So, next in line was my twin, Khalil and I to pursue a post-secondary education.

My final semester as a high school student, I still didn't know where I would spend the next four years. What made matters worse was that, I was a student athlete, with no scouting interest or film to send to college coaches. The women's basketball coaching staff was extremely unstable. At the time, I was struggling to build a relationship with my third coach in a four-year period. It almost felt like I was introduced to a new coach each year. As an athlete, that is not is not a good feeling- Coach Martin was the last coach I had before I went off to college. Now, we may have had a love/hate relationship, but she was indeed one of the best coaches I'd ever had during my 15 plus years as an athlete. If you're reading this, thank you for believing in me.

Time was winding down. I knew I had to go somewhere to continue my passion. Of course, my education was most important. But if it weren't for basketball, I don't think college would have been an option for me. My dad always told me that college would be some of the best years of my life. He was right. As a matter of fact, if I could describe my college experience in two words, it would be: *motion picture.* So, there I was, an eighteen-year-old girl from Atlanta, Georgia attending an HBCU out of state, hours away from the place I called home and thousands of miles away from relatives. I was slightly nervous leaving everything behind, but I was also extremely anxious to see what the future held for me. New experiences. New opportunities. New friends. Overall, it was a new beginning.

I remember it like it was yesterday. I moved into first college dorm room and met my first college roommate. I met my first college best friend on the outside basketball court and started in my first collegiate basketball game. I met my first college boyfriend and experienced one of many heartbreaks. From enjoying my first college party, to experiencing my first and last time "sloppy drunk" moment and attending my first college Homecoming, college was so much more than an experience. I even went from not having a clue about sororities and fraternities to becoming a member of Alpha Kappa Alpha Sorority, Incorporated. But never in five-year tenure at Morris College, did I expect to become an HBCU Campus Queen.

For me, it was one of those, "Expect the unexpected" moments. It was during my senior year, when Santana, a classmate of mine, decided to make a bet with me to become a part of the Student Government Association.

"If I run for SGA President, you have to run for Miss Morris College, Santana requested."

I laughed jokingly and accepted the challenge. I honestly thought he was just joking until he approached me with the application form a few days later. At that moment, I knew I could not flake out of the bet. Once approved from the Dean of Student Affairs, it was time to connect with the student body through our creative campaigns. Within a week of campaigning, Santana no longer wanted to participate in the race, leaving me no choice but to follow through with my word. As word got around campus that I was running for Queen, students told me how great of an idea it was and how much I had their support. I knew at that moment that, I couldn't continue to treat it as just a bet.

I continued to promote myself by posting flyers and hosting small events on campus. Then came speech night. I was up against five other beautiful women. My adrenaline was pumping through the roof due to my fear of public speaking. Maybe it was the support from my fellow classmates that kept me from panicking and eventually walking off the stage. Or it was the anxiety of reciting Marianne Williamson's inspiring poem, "Our Deepest Fear" during my speech. From that day forward, I had no idea that my college experience would change forever.

It was a Friday, I walked out of the Wilson Booker Science Building and received many phone calls, one of which was from the current campus Queen at that time.

"Congratulations Miss Morris College! Kenyetta said, with her voice full of joy." There were so many unexplainable feelings going through my head when I received the great news. How did I, a sweatpants-wearing, shy and introverted, student athlete, who never even ran for prom queen in high school, win a position as important as Miss Morris College? It was given moment, that I realized I had more to offer than just my athleticism. I was no longer just the pretty girl who played sports. I was now Lakil Mason, the 63rd Miss Morris College. I was officially held to a much higher standard and utopian perspective. I was now a public figure of my institution. That meant that my every move was being documented. In other words, I could not get caught slipping in any shape or form. That was the number one rule of being a Queen.

However, one thing people tend to forget when in a leadership position is that you are human before anything else. I couldn't give them the "perfect" Queen they wanted. I had to learn to balance my personal life and relationships with academics, athletics and work. If I'm being completely transparent, the last two years of my five-year matriculation at Morris College were the most challenging. I was a broke college student. My grade point average fluctuated. My relationship with my basketball coach was unpredictable. My father was arrested a few months after my coronation ceremony, resulting in his absence at my graduation. But not all things were bad.

Within those two years, I strengthened relationships with my professors and mentors. I landed an internship opportunity that contributed to my first full-time job after college. And, most importantly, I became a first-generation college graduate. Overall, college is indeed a humbling experience. If you haven't tried it, don't knock it until you do. I've met some pretty amazing people along the way, some who have become lifelong friends. If I could experience it all again, I would. Becoming Miss Morris brought me out of my comfort zone. That's when I discovered even greater things about myself.

I was no longer the shy, soft-spoken girl from Atlanta. I was no longer afraid to speak in front of large crowds. I was no longer afraid to be my authentic self around people. One thing I learned about myself during my reign as Miss Morris College is to never speak perfection. No matter what pedestal you are put on, a perfect person does not exist. Rule number one in life: Always show up as your authentic self. Some people will like you for who you are, and others won't. Either way, that's okay. Your job on this Earth is to be happy. The other part is to live in your purpose. My purpose in life is to inspire. Morris College helped me realized that.

As students, our goal was the enter to learn, depart to serve. I am forever grateful for my HBCU. Looking back, I never imagined being included in the Miss Morris College lineage and being the last Queen to serve under the longest serving president in HBCU history. I never imagined joining a black sorority. Never imagined completing college with a Bachelor of Science. Never imagined being the one to set the foundation for college graduates in my family. Never limit yourself to the things you can achieve in life. Anything is possible, as long as you believe in *you*.

About Lakil Mason

Lakil Mason was born in Greenville, North Carolina and raised in Atlanta, Georgia. She is the only the daughter of five children to Stacy Lucas and Leonard Mason.

Lakil attended the public schools of Cobb County, graduating from South Cobb High School in 2013. Later that year, she enrolled to the illustrious Morris College on a basketball scholarship. During her matriculation, she reached many milestones including the following: earning the title of the 63rd Miss Morris College, becoming a member of Alpha Kappa Alpha Sorority, Incorporated and receiving a Bachelor's of Science Degree.

Lakil has always been known for her hard work, athleticism, great leadership and positive spirit. After graduating, she landed a full-time job in her profession as a Wastewater Laboratory Analyst. She was also able to reconnect with a former basketball coach who trusted her with an opportunity to join The Village Market ATL. Within just two years of doing the work, Lakil was promoted to Executive Assistant of the company. The Village Market has opened up many opportunities and connections for her; that is why she will forever stress the importance of building relationships.

In addition to expanding her professional portfolio, she is currently aiming to pursue her lifelong passion for modeling and acting. Lakil's ultimate goal is to become a household name through entertainment, philanthropy, education and mentorship. She believes her patience, dedication, character, leadership, and humbleness will guide her on the path to success.

CHELSEA JOHNSON

Redefining the Queen

Chelsea Johnson

Miss Livingstone College 2008-2009

"I don't care how dark the night. I believe in the coming of the morning."

These were words spoken by the late Joseph C. Price, founder and the first President of Livingstone College. Words that whisper constantly in my conscience to help guide the footsteps of this proud Blue Bear and 2008-2009 Miss Livingstone College. These words molded me and laid the foundation that would prepare me for my now season.

Choosing Livingstone College to extend my education was an easy decision. I was able to enter into an educational community where God was at the center and I was able to continue playing basketball. It never occurred to me that God would have an additional calling and purpose on my life. The titled event, "An Evening of Unveiled Cache'," would begin my reign as Miss Livingstone College, but it also unveiled the calling on my life to take the road less traveled.

One month before the deadline to enter the Miss Livingstone College Race, I was playing in a basketball game. The next thing I remembered was being transported to the hospital by ambulance. A junior guard for the women's basketball team, healthy and extremely fit, I would have never imagined that something could be wrong with me. After being transported to the emergency room and released later that night, I began experiencing migraines daily. Seeking medical treatment became a consistent activity that I had to endure, searching for answers that I thought would never come. After weeks of continuous testing, I was admitted into the hospital for exploratory procedures. After a few days, a doctor came in the room to tell me that a scan revealed that I had a brain aneurysm.

A choice is defined as an act of selecting or making a decision when faced with two or more possibilities. The choice I had was to select an operation, which had several negative side effects, or choose the watch-and-wait approach while continuing to take medication. Neither of these choices were ideal, nor were they something that anyone should ever have to choose. However, one thing I learned that day was that, in the midst of adversity, you discover how strong you truly are. Not only does adversity reveal strength, but it also places many things in perspective. I contemplated running for Miss Livingstone College, and I heard many of my peers suggest it just the same. However, it wasn't until that very moment with doctors and family asking me what my choice was *medically* did I learn what my choice was *spiritually*.

I chose to watch and wait. I chose to take medication that would help prevent growth or rupture of the aneurysm. I was released from the hospital and immediately went back to campus to turn in my packet to become Miss Livingstone College. Through campaigning and speaking with the student body, it was clear that God began to work on me. Every day, it became clearer that God had chosen me and the battles that I faced to lead my peer., He chose me to be His vessel for that time. I was crowned Miss Livingstone College, and it was one of the happiest moments of my life.

My reign taught me a myriad of lessons that helped shape me into the person I am today. One of those lessons hit harder than the others. "Never allow anyone to define who you are. You control the narrative of your own life." I can remember it so clearly. At the beginning of my reign, I was invited to several programs and events. Once individuals who were connected to the institution found out that the current Miss Livingstone was a ball player, it sparked an excitement that no one expected. It was new. It was not the status quo. It proved that a queen has multiple definitions. Leaving practice one day and rushing to my apartment to change for an event, I was stopped by a few of my peers. They were noticeably upset. When I asked them what was wrong, they told me that they overhead someone who was in an important position state that they did not know how they felt about a "tomboy" being Miss Livingstone College.

My immediate instinct was to put their minds at ease. As I got to the room and prepared for the event, I thought more and more on their words.

They bothered me for a moment. But then I realized that I was in a position to change minds and effect change. It would have been easy to nurse my feelings and harp on what was said about me. However, I learned that the only person who could define who I was would be me. I realized that the beauty of being a queen was realizing that there was no single layer of definition.

A queen embodies grace and awareness. She is multifaceted. It was in that moment that I stood taller. I vowed to take that negative energy and allow it to push me further. Never allow someone to tell you what you can or cannot become.

Being an HBCU Queen while also being the starting point guard for the women's basketball team taught me the meaning of balance. While serving in these roles, I had to continue to uphold a high academic standard. Scholarship was the main goal and academics always came first. This translated even in my current position as an educator and girls' basketball coach. Each year, I teach and mold future doctors, lawyers, engineers, scientists and world leaders in all forms. I speak to them often about my previous roles and positions. Not only do I speak to them, but I lead by action. Learning balance helped me earn a Master of Education in Educational Leadership with a 4.0 GPA. I did this while teaching full-time in the midst of basketball season. My experiences as an HBCU Queen gave me the necessary tools to accomplish amazing feats, even when I had to maintain a heavy workload.

The Word of God tells us in Philippians 1:6, *We can be certain of this, that he who began a good work in you will carry it on to completion until the day of Christ Jesus.* While Miss Livingstone College, God showed me that we are all here for a reason. I found my reasons when I was installed as Miss Livingstone College. That same calling continues to lead me daily. It has helped me facilitate a weekly *Servant Leadership* Session with coaches and leaders where we speak about God's Word and how to become better individuals and leaders. There was a time when I would have harvested my ideas. There were moments when I sat on dreams and plans because I did not want the spotlight. As an HBCU Queen, I learned that the spotlight was only as beneficial as the one standing in it. What do you do when the light is shining upon you? Every day I continue to hear, "Let your light so shine." Then, I recalled this same message in my campaign for Miss Livingstone College. I promised to be a ray of sunshine for Livingstone College. That promise is one that I continue to make in my daily walk.

Life is a journey of highs and lows. Both equally shape us into the individuals we are today and who we will become. I am so thankful that each high and low, each ebb and flow, equipped me with what I needed to become—not only an HBCU Queen—but a lifelong queen. As a lifelong queen, my best advice for anyone is to learn who you are for yourself so that no one else can define you. It is the single most beautiful attribute to be so rooted in who you are that no one can reshape or veer you off of your path.

When I chose Livingstone College to further my education, I enrolled with the plan to play basketball and obtain a degree. However, I received so much more. I was crowned Miss Livingstone College 2008-2009 and became an HBCU Queen. The tools and lessons I learned allow me to aim as high as my heels but remain as humble and grounded as my crossover. The people who I was able to reach help me continue to learn the value in relationships. The crown that I wore helped me learn that heavy is the head that wears it, but mighty is the head that seeks crown from the kingdom of God.

"I don't care how dark the night. I believe in the coming of the morning."

The words that guided me in my walk as an HBCU Queen and in each basketball season. The words that guide me in my walk as a lifelong queen and my *now* season.

About Chelsea Johnson

Chelsea F. Johnson Muir is an Educator and the Head Girls Basketball Coach at Amos P. Godby High School in Tallahassee, Florida. Here, she teaches Biology, Physical Science and Advance Placement Environmental Science. She has taught for seven years and has coached for eleven years.

Chelsea is a 2005 Alumna of Amos P. Godby High School, which is what motivates her to mold young people, daily. Along with teaching and coaching, she championed "Cougar Kings," a program geared towards the development and mentoring of young men. Chelsea believes that all students want to learn and be successful; they just need guidance, love and someone to believe in them. Through education, Chelsea was awarded as the 2017 Distinguished Educator of the Year, and was named one of the Top Educators of America, 2019-2020 by The Who's Who Directories.

Chelsea holds a Bachelor of Science in Biology and a minor in Chemistry from Livingstone College. Here, she was a Four-Year Letter winner and Point Guard for the Lady Blue Bears Women's Basketball Team. She graduated with honors and reigned as Miss Livingstone College 2008-2009. She also holds a Master of Education in Educational Leadership from Louisiana State University-Shreveport where she graduated with a 4.0 Grade Point Average.

Chelsea is a member of various organizations. She is a member of Delta Sigma Theta Sorority, Incorporated, The National Society of Leadership and Success, The Florida Athletic Coaches Association, and The Coaches' Coalition. In 2019, Chelsea was inducted into the Association of Godby Graduates Hall of Fame in the Athletics Category, for her hard work and successful career in sports.

Chelsea is the creator of *The Coaches Bible Study,* which is a Servant Leadership guided webinar session for coaches and leaders to learn how to better serve those that we lead. This endeavor has allowed her to speak with numerous collegiate coaches and professionals about their views of Servant Leadership, and how they apply it to their current roles.

Chelsea is a member of Tabernacle Missionary Baptist Church in Tallahassee, Florida. Here she sings in the church's United Voices Mass Choir, and the Young Adult Chorale. Her faith is the most important thing to her. Being a Brain Aneurysm Survivor fuels her faith and goal of sharing the word of God to whomever may listen.

Chelsea was born in Marietta, Georgia and raised in both Tallahassee and Midway, Florida. She is the daughter of Vicki Muse Johnson and the granddaughter of the late James and Earnestine Muse of Midway, Florida. She is married to Alwayne Muir.

JESSICA NATHAN BROWN

When Dreams Become Reality

Jessica Nathan Brown

Miss Stillman College 2012-2013

As a little girl, I looked forward to browsing the pages of the *HBCU Campus Queens* edition of *Ebony Magazine* every year. Flipping through those pages made me excited and empowered. I knew from an early age that I wanted to attend an HBCU. One of my goals was to become a campus Queen. I wanted to serve my institution and inspire young girls like those Queens had done for me. Who knew this dream would come true? Fast forward to freshman year at Stillman College in Tuscaloosa, Alabama, where my classmates began signing up for the Miss Freshman Competition, which took place during orientation week. I got excited about signing up, but then fear overcame me.

So many thoughts ran through my head. *Who's going to vote for me? I'm nervous to get up in front of people who I've only met a few days ago to perform a talent. I won't win.* With these thoughts swarming around in my head, I did not sign up to participate. The crazy part is that I have always been a person to go after what I wanted, no matter if I won or lost. But I was so afraid to go after this venture. As I reflect on that experience, I think entering a new phase of my life as a college student away from home brought pressure that I wasn't expecting. As I sat through the Miss Freshman Competition a few days later, I kept questioning whether I'd made the right decision. Regardless, it was too late. All I could do was go after any future opportunities without fear.

My next campus Queen opportunity came leading up to my junior year when I found out that one of the residence halls was looking for someone to represent them for the 2011- 2012 year. I jumped at the opportunity to become Miss Knox Hall. It was a great decision not only to represent the residence hall, but to also become a member of the Campus Queens Association. This allowed me to learn more about the organization and to get to know the current Miss Stillman College. All the women who had served as Miss Stillman during my time so far were great, but I didn't have a chance to get to know them personally. Having the opportunity to work with Miss Stillman 2012-2013 was amazing. She was caring, friendly and passionate. She carried herself with so much class. I enjoyed conversations with her, and she quickly became like a big sister to me. She was a great role model on campus.

I got more excited about running at the end of the following spring semester. Before I knew it, the applications were available for Miss Stillman 2012-2013, and there was no doubt in my mind about applying. Unlike freshman year, I was excited, confident, and ready for this journey, no matter the outcome. Even if I did not win, I would not have any regrets about competing for the title of Miss Stillman. I brainstormed campaign slogans and ideas for activities to encourage my peers to vote for me. I decided to run on the platform, "Because You're Worth It: Discovering Your Inner Self" to promote positive self-image and confidence in young women. I wanted to empower young Black women to believe in themselves, realize their abilities, and recognize their worth.

I did not have a lot of money to spend. So, I had to be creative with my campaign materials and events. My stepdad took my photos for my flyers and other materials. In addition to ordering buttons and ink pens, I bought a spool of blank CDs and created a playlist of popular 90s music to pass out to fellow students. I used my laptop to burn the playlist onto CDs, placed labels with my name and slogan on each one, and placed them into white CD envelopes. I was proud of what I was able to accomplish with a small budget and my classmates seemed to like my choice of songs, too. I also hosted a few small events to answer questions for students to get to know me better. I learned that it didn't matter so much about how much money I spent or how nice the giveaways were. It was about the person. It was about exemplifying the qualities of a Stillman woman, someone who was genuine, humble, passionate, relatable. Someone who was a leader.

The competition began with an interview with the panel of judges. I walked into my interview extremely nervous, but I kept it together and answered the questions to the best of my ability. On pageant day, five amazing women and I competed for the title of Miss Stillman College. My friend, also named Jessica, and I whispered encouraging words to each other before heading on stage. It was a great feeling having women lift each other up and to remove stereotypes that pageants receive about backstage drama.

At one point, I couldn't remember the first word of my speech as I stood on the side of the stage. Then, my name was called. I walked out with a smile and prayed that the words would come to me. I stood in front of the microphone and, somehow, the words flowed. The pageant went by so quickly and everyone did a great job. I knew it was going to be tough and started having doubts. I mentally prepared myself just in case I lost. I kept telling myself that I had a good chance of winning first or second runner-up, and I was okay with that. For some reason, I couldn't think of myself actually winning at that time. I waited two more days for the winner to be announced during the annual Student Choice Awards. Two of my sorority sisters teased me, telling me that I would probably remain seated with a dainty clap if I won because of my reserved personality.

On the night of the event, I sat nervously through the ceremony. Once all the awards were announced, it was finally time to announce the winner. Dr. Whittaker-Davis, the Vice President of Student Affairs and advisor to Miss Stillman, began with second runner-up, calling my sorority sister Victoria's name. Then she called Jessica's name as the first runner-up. I crumbled a little inside, honestly thinking that I did not place at all. Then, Dr. Whittaker-Davis called my name as Miss Stillman College 2012-2013. All I remember is sitting there softly clapping as my mom and everyone else around me jumped up and down, screaming. I don't think it really hit me until the next day.

I came back from summer break, eager to start my reign as Miss Stillman beginning with hosting the Miss Freshman Pageant that I was too afraid to participate in my first year. Working with Dr. Whittaker-Davis as my advisor was a very rewarding experience. She gave me great advice and really allowed me to do things my way. She was very receptive to all the ideas that I wanted to implement. Having a mentor who supports you, as well as challenges you, is important. I am forever grateful for her.

I have so many great memories. I will never forget how great it felt when the crowd cheered as I walked around to the home side of the football field with the SGA officers during halftime of the first game. During homecoming, I enjoyed the annual Miss Stillman Tea with the other campus Queens hosted by the college's first lady and the Blue Pride Luncheon. I was excited to ride on a float with my royal court in the homecoming parade and to be introduced on the fifty-yard line during halftime. I also went to elementary and middle schools to read to kids and crown young girls during their coronations.

My experience also taught me how to be adaptable. One challenge was learning that the renovations in the gym, where coronations were traditionally held, would not be done in time to host mine. So, we pushed it to November during homecoming. I was nervous yet hopeful. In the end, everything worked out, and my coronation was held at The Bama Theatre, where we presented Miss Stillman in The Wiz. Yes, I was a little over the top with production, but I love every second of it!

One of my priorities was to continue the work of the former Miss Stillman by investing time and energy into the Campus Queens Association. Building relationships with the Queens on campus was important to me, and I hoped to make a positive impact on my sister Queens. We hosted tabling events to promote different initiatives and hosted an event for young girls to come to campus to discuss how to be confident and empower one another. We hosted one of the pep rallies, campus Queen-style, where we played games that included giving students a chance to pie a campus Queen. We were more than our crowns, and we were not afraid to be active. We were a well-rounded group and wanted to represent Stillman to the best of our ability.

During the spring semester, the time came to record my video submission for the campus Queen edition of *Ebony Magazine*, which now features the Top 10 Queens in the magazine based on online votes. Although I did not receive enough votes to be included in the magazine, I was still honored to submit my video to be included on the website among the other amazing HBCU Queens sharing our experiences with the world. I was afforded so many wonderful opportunities as Miss Stillman. I returned to participate in activities like the Miss Stillman Tea and coronation over the next few years after my reign. Being a campus Queen was a privilege, and it was such an honor to serve as the ambassador for my beloved alma mater. I am thankful that the judges and my peers believed that I could represent Stillman College well. My year as Miss Stillman was one of the best experiences of my life. I hope I was able to leave a legacy of good leadership, positive relationships, and, most importantly, empowering young women.

I believe the journey is just as important as the destination. My journey to becoming Miss Stillman proved that dreams do come true and pushed me to serve with passion and humility. Serving as Miss Stillman helped mold me into the woman I am today. My experience gave me the confidence and skills to make an impact on young women and men through my job, my sorority activities, and my involvement at church. My hope is that current and future campus Queens will be an inspiration for young women and men like those who inspired me. I pray they will embrace the journey and strive to make a positive impact on their campuses and communities because we all have so much to offer.

We are more than our crowns.

We are confident leaders.

We are powerful Black women.

We are HBCU Queens.

About Jessica Nathan Brown

Jessica Nathan Brown is a native of Birmingham, Alabama. She is currently the Assistant Director of Student Activities in the Office of Student Involvement & Leadership at the University of Alabama at Birmingham. Jessica graduated summa cum laude from Stillman College in Tuscaloosa, Alabama with a Bachelor of Arts in Psychology, where she served as Miss Stillman College 2012-2013. She received a Master of Education in Educational Leadership from the University of South Alabama.

Jessica is happily married to her husband Brandon. She is very involved in activities at Macedonia Missionary Baptist Church, and she is a member of Delta Sigma Theta Sorority, Inc. and student affairs professional organizations. In her spare time, Jessica enjoys spending time with her family and friends, singing, reading, and watching movies.

DEBORAH RICHARDSON PRICE

Evolution of a Queen

Deborah Richardson Price

Miss North Carolina A&T State University 1977-1978

Attendants/Escorts:

Karen Ravenell (Senior)/Donny Simmons; Deborah Wiley (Junior)/Sam Ferguson; Patricia Maye (Sophomore)/Terrence Marable; Greta Shaw (Freshman)/Bill McComb; Robert Richardson (Miss NCATSU Escort/Brother)

Student Government Executive Board:

Tony Graham (President); Warren 'Toby' Bryant (Vice President); Cynthia McMurray (Secretary); Curtis Askew (Treasurer); Clark McGriff (Sergeant at Arms, President Assistant); Pierre Melvin (Public Relations); Mike Davis (Attorney General)

Forty-six years ago, my mother drove down to the North Carolina Agricultural and Technical State University (NCATSU) campus. She helped set up my dorm room, then left me standing in the High Rise dormitory parking lot. My father was stationed in Thailand at the time and could not make the trip. Before leaving, she whispered in my ear, "Now your journey begins. Trust in your walk and you'll be okay."

I didn't quite understand what she meant. But *now* I do.

I didn't realize what lied ahead for me on my path or what direction this journey would take me.

I had the power to make my own decisions. and hold myself accountable for my actions moving forward. With my parents' words in the back of my mind: "Strive! Do your best and just *be.*", I had a new outlook on how I would approach my college experience

Initially the journey was rough because I didn't know anyone, nor did I know what to expect. and had little to no money. I had no clue who my roommate was, didn't know which way to go or how to get there. This was my first experience of going through life on my own.

Like a typical freshman, I experienced the highs and lows – partying, socializing, and trying to figure out the whole 'class scheduling' thing. I was trying to navigate my own space in a place that felt so large and overwhelming. I quickly found myself going in a direction that was not the path I wanted to be on.. I wasn't performing to the best of my abilities and ended up in academic trouble. I felt like I let myself down but, more importantly, the people who believed in me. I specifically remembered the shock of my first GPA being *1.98*. But what stuck with me most was the look of disappointment on my mother's face when she saw that GPA. In that moment, I knew something had to change. I had a decision to make: "Do what it takes to make it *or* fail and go home."

Needless to say, I got my second chance to get things right.

The four years that were spent both on and off the campus grounds helped mold me into the person I am today.

I cultivated and maintained endearing relationships; discovered both creative and survival skills; and, participated in various extracurricular activities. I also joined various organizations; became a student counselor; and took the time to realize the power of the seeds that were planted in me.

Freshman Year

I met the person who would become one of my best friends during my freshman year. We were the 'first' and 'last' people to register for our business courses. We both didn't have a clue! Karen Ravenell was not only a best friend, but she was my Miss A&T Senior Attendant. She is family to this very day..

Working in the cafeteria was one of my main sources of income through the work study program. Our primary responsibility was to feed the Aggie Family food, but it became more of a bonding experience when we fed them emotionally and spiritually. I watched as Ms. Laura Thornton, our 'Cafeteria Mom,' used her discerning ear and fed us as if she were at home in her kitchen. It had to be right! We were feeding her babies! This was one of my first lesson in appreciating what service truly meant.

One of my most memorable experiences was when I tried out and made the cheerleading squad. This four-year relationship was more than cheerleading; these people became my family. We were more than thighs and hips; we were strong women and men with a voice. Our voices represented the school both on and off the field during football as well as at home and away on the courts for basketball Our voices even gave us the courage to walk on the Chancellor's house to rally for student rights.

We proudly accompanied the Blue and Gold Marching Machine, a band that was second to none! In state and out of state, we represented NCATSU. We cheered, marched, stomped, walked, cried, laughed, played, sang, protested, prayed, and represented the university as "one body, one family."

Sophomore Year

My primary focus during my sophomore year was on academics. I had a lot of ground to cover! However, barely getting through Biology class was truly a challenge. I had problems dissecting that frog! Through it all, grades rose significantly and *so did my GPA*!

I was chosen to represent my class as Miss Sophomore and was actively engaged with the cheerleading squad, pep club, softball team and even a member of the Alobeaem Club.

Junior Year

One of the biggest honors bestowed on me during my junior year was when I had the privilege to represent the Omega Psi Phi Fraternity as Miss Mu Psi. I was truly humbled by the brothers of purple and gold. My bond with the fraternity was, and continues to be, a special, endearing one to this very day.

Additional activities included participating on the Aggie Softball Team, acting as a student counselor, and joining the Business Administration Club.

Then came “THAT MOMENT”; the moment I became Miss A&T. In the spring of 1977, I remember walking by the Omega plot with a glove on my head, carrying cleats, and covered in dirt. I was not yet aware of the outcome of the Miss A&T election, but I was anxiously awaiting the results. Then suddenly, everyone burst out of their cars and the dorms screaming, “You won! You won!” Students literally came from everywhere and everyone celebrated and embraced me with love for my moment. This moment felt so much bigger than me. It was a culmination of three years of building a community and surrounding myself with love that I knew I had to do something special for. It was in that moment that I promised I would give the student body a gift of gratitude for bestowing such an honor onto me. I was simply speechless.

During the summer months before returning to campus for my senior year, I gave myself an assignment to research our history, embrace the ‘HBCU Why’ and be the voice of the student body. I discovered during my research a *true* appreciation for the rich history behind the school and what the *real* Aggie experience was all about.

Senior Year

My bond with the university, student body, the administration and student government executive team (‘The Cabinet’) strengthened on so many levels during my senior year. As I learned about the rich history of A&T, and the cultural significance of what it meant to this country, it made it easier to articulate what the school meant to the student body. Learning of the events during the Civil Rights Movement, which included the infamous sit-in at “The Woolworth Counter” that changed the course of history. The bullets in Scott Hall wall that were retained and memorialized symbolized the riots that happened on campus. The blood stains on the sidewalks symbolized how people gave their lives and died for their rights on campus and more.

I grew to have a true appreciation of the 'HBCU Why' and the contributory role that North Carolina A&T State University played, and continues to play, for so many.

> **"HBCU Why"** - For those doors closed to minorities, HBCUs opened their door, enabling access to a college education and providing a supportive environment to succeed.
>
> *"HBCUs may sit in different pews; but WE ALL BELONG TO THE SAME CHURCH – **FAMILY**."*

I then reflected on a conversation with Michelle Burney (*'my first'* Miss A&T-1974 my freshman year). I gained a greater understanding of her words of advice and examples of excellence. Her emphasis on carrying yourself with pride, grace, class, and dignity were all a testament of why she reigned supreme and was an influence in my life.

I took it upon myself to follow in her footsteps by fully immersing myself in the Aggie experience. My class schedule was fully supplemented with the endless university presentations and appearances, working as a student counselor, and serving as a "Student Government Cabinet" member.

The Student Government Association (SGA) was masterfully led by Tony Graham, SGA President (currently a professor at A&T). His cabinet embodied a dynamic collaboration of classmates. We had a connection that was indescribable. We collectively understood what A&T was all about and we wanted to do something that was unforgettable. We *collectively* felt the honor of holding our respective positions as 'Agents' of the university. This was *personal.* We walked, cried, laughed, prayed, sang, and planned as a collective *family*. We were the *voice* and *face* of the student body and we *wanted to represent*. We did just that!

We wanted to express our appreciation to the student body for their belief and trust in our works. Our homecoming theme was appropriately titled, "Coming Home with a Touch of Class".

We created an environment that not only accommodated the alumni, but that represented the student body in the best way possible. It was designed to let their hair down and feel the love of our *entire* Aggie Family. The song lyrics to "Home" as sung by Stephanie Mills depicts our call to our alumni.

It was time for them to come to that place. That place called 'Home.' And they did just that! It was a celebration!

As a bonus, we decided to give the university a unique gift. A gift that no one has been able to top to this day. It was a live concert during coronation featuring the iconic artist of Melba Moore.

Chancellor Dowdy looked at us and asked, "How did you all do that?"

We simply said, "Don't worry. It was legal."

Needless to say, the 1977-1978 academic year was a time to remember.

Jessie Jackson and Ron McNair, two Aggie Icons, came 'Home' to honor and celebrate our fellow Aggies as they graduated. We stood side by side. It was a proud moment in history.

You see, my reign *wasn't* about '*"ME"*. It was about "WE". It was an accumulation of a four -year journey, which symbolized an endless 'Thank you' to all those who crossed my path while on A&T's campus grounds. The students, the professors, the administration, the counselors, the various teams (both academic and athletic), the organizations, the Blue and Gold Marching Machine; and the *cheerleaders*. Those who entrusted me with the honor to represent the student body. Those who trusted me to carry and symbolize the Aggie legacy. Those who trusted me to be their voice and carry the torch of the 'HBCU Why'. Most importantly, those who entrusted me to stand for those who once stood and are now lying down.

This will be a journey that I will never forget!

So, you may ask, what *my* experience taught me that I would like to pass on to future Queens?

- Tenacity
- Humility
- Work Ethic
- Appreciate Professors' Tough Love
- Service
- Never Give Up
- Power of the Voice
- Family
- Endear Alliances
- Home
- Setbacks Are Successes in Reverse
- Never Underestimate, but Believe in Yourself
- Excellence
- *Aggie Pride*

The most important lesson that I would like to instill in you all is, "Appreciate your past, embrace your today, trust in your tomorrow."

Trust in your journey, even if you can't see the finish line. Keep pedaling. You never know who or what is waiting for you. And always remember that you'll *never* walk alone.

About Deborah Richardson Price

Ms. Price currently resides in Willingboro, NJ and works as a Bank Regulatory Compliance Executive in the NY Metropolitan Area. She entered into the banking industry once leaving NCATSU in 1978 and amassed years of industry, audit, regulatory, business knowledge as well as strong leadership and relational skillsets that enables her to manage and govern regulatory compliance across the largest domestic and international financial enterprises.

Her experience spans multiple regulatory disciplines which are essential acquiring information about the latest news and research in regulatory technology, risk management and cybersecurity industries within financial services.

With over 30+ years of Compliance and Auditing experience, 11 years of service had been garnered on the federal level as a National Bank Examiner with the Comptroller of the Currency and three years as a Compliance Examiner in the Supervision and Regulation Department of the Federal Reserve Bank of Philadelphia. She is proficient in both the investigation; evaluation; quality assurance, and, implementation of corrective measures of bank irregularities

Ms. Price has served as Regulatory Compliance Officer (RCO); Regulation Coordinator /Subject Matter Expert (SME); Managed Divisional Compliance Officers; Regulatory/Compliance Liaison for International Representative Office(s); Bank Secrecy Act/Anti-Money Laundering Act (BSA/AML) Officer; Privacy Officer; and Community Reinvestment Act (CRA) Officer for five financial institutions.

Among her prior duties, she has served as Regulatory Liaison Officer (RLO) for domestic and global commercial businesses where she managed relationships with regulatory authorities, to include information management; coordinated and supervised oversight of the examination processes; managing meetings; and, conducted investigations.

Civic, Community, Domestic and International Arenas.

Ms. Price sustains an extensive record in civic, community, domestic and international arenas.

Some of her prior experiences have given her the opportunity to serve as Director for Compliance with several banks; Community Reinvestment Act (CRA) Officer for five financial institutions where she developed internal CRA plans to ensure compliance with regulations and maintained public files. Managed and conducted community outreach efforts to ascertain community needs, identified CRA opportunities for meeting community development lending, services and investment needs.; as well as, serve as an Executive Director for a Faith-based Community Development Corporation in New Jersey.

SeedsFoundation Inc. (Founder) - Ms. Price established the **SeedsFoundation Inc...** A 'behind the scenes' organization designed to touch the lives of children enabling the unimaginable resources and experiences happen which often plant life-changing 'seeds' that will be paid forward.

World of Money, Inc (WOM) (Board of Director/ Chairperson) - WOM founded in 2005, is a New York City based 501(c)(3) non-profit organization whose mission is to empower youth with a sound financial education. This program has broken generational cycles and changed the way youth and their parents understand their money. Its immersive curriculum equips children with five tenets for a financially responsible and philanthropic life: learn, earn, save, invest and donate. Financial presenters are stellar Wall Street professionals, business and legal leaders.

Via 24 coalition partners, the World of Money provides youth with our unique youth financial education mobile app. This app is currently being utilized by these national, local, regional and global organizations in Senegal, Ghana, South Africa, China, India and Rwanda.

Nnabagereka Development Foundation (NDF)/ (U.S. Advisory Council) - Ms. Price serves on the U.S. Advisory Council for the Nnabagereka Development Foundation. The NDF is a registered non-governmental organization founded in 2000 by **Her Royal Highness the Nnabagereka (Queen) of Buganda, Sylvia Nagginda**.

Founded in 2000, NDF has actively been involved in making a positive difference in the lives of children, women and youth in Uganda. NDF it draws on the positive cultural values from the rich cultural background of the Kingdom of Buganda and balances the mixture of traditional and contemporary values to make a difference not only at the national level but at the international level as well.

Education Africa (EA) (United States/ Board Member – Advisory Council).

Ms. Price serves as a Board Member/Advisory Council for Education Africa. She has been affiliated with Education Africa since 2010. Established in 1992, Education Africa strives to reach and uplift the poorest of the poor. With education as the cornerstone for all projects, EA aims to assist disadvantaged South Africans in their quest to obtain a quality, relevant education in order to ensure that they are in a position to become global citizens and a competitive, productive element in the local job market. Education Africa aims for an educated nation, which in turn will lead to a progressive nation that is able to sustain economic growth.

Professional Affiliation(s): List available upon request.

Greek Affiliation: Delta Sigma Theta

Civic Affiliations: Willingboro Township Committeewomen

Neighborhood Watch (Block Captain)

Emergency Response Teams (Willingboro Township & Burlington County)

Church Affiliation: Bethany Baptist Church, Lindenwold, NJ

Bishop David G Evans

Ministries: Missionary, Nursing

Children: Thomas Price, Kyle Price, Tiffany Price-Bond (Greg Bond)

Grandchildren: Nasir Bond, Jaylan Bond, Imani Bond

SHARTAJEYE' WRIGHT

Jewels of Wisdom

Shartajeye' Wright

Miss Texas Southern University 2011-2012

As a campus queen, there were many stages to grace embellished in elaborate suits and dresses. The crown was opulent, and it attracted a lot of attention. There were countless opportunities to acquire first-class treatment and activate access to exclusive events with university officials and celebrities. Many often assumed that your role was limited to a university figurehead, someone who is just meant to sit and look pretty while exhibiting the best of manners. While I was able to exceed the expectations of exhibiting regality, that was just the tip of the iceberg as it related to my intentionality to re-shape the perspective of a campus queen.

Two years prior to winning the title, I came across someone who seemed to only limit their impact to the title alone. One afternoon after a Student Government Association meeting, I met the then reigning Miss Texas Southern and, ironically, that's exactly how she introduced herself. The tall, slender, well-dressed woman extended her hand and stated, "Hello, I'm Miss Texas Southern University."

After a brief pause, I extended my hand and asked, "Okay, so what's your name?" Although we joke about it today, at that moment, I noticed that the title could either give you an identity or give you a platform to activate your purpose. After my brief interaction with the queen two years prior to my reign, I instantly thought, *I can do this.* The motivation to become Miss Texas Southern University was my newfound "why" as a recent transfer student.

My platform, Project GREATNESS, is still relevant in my life today as an educator, influencer and community organizer as I advocate for educational equity for children in my city. Buck Roger's quote still pierces every time read it: "There are countless ways of achieving greatness, but any road to achieving one's maximum potential must be built on a bedrock of respect for the individual, a commitment to excellence, and a rejection of mediocrity." As a campus queen, I learned that my platform was more about how I chose to elevate the concerns of others who did not have access to the table where I had a reserved seat. Achieving greatness often tests your character and mental strength. It isolates you in the midst of a large crowd. It's a daring prompt to tread the unknown in an effort to achieve the unimaginable. It's ironic how society praises trailblazers long after they pass away. Yet, when they were blazing the trail, the person was often persecuted and isolated.

My journey as a campus queen taught me how to endure the heaviness of leadership, while still keeping a smile on my face in the midst of what may have felt like an internal storm. I am quite aware that I may have painted a "less glorious" portrayal of my reign. In all honesty, others assume that the opulent stones contribute to the weight of the crown. On the contrary, it is the weight of the responsibility that makes the journey more meaningful. A royal journey cultivated the reason for my mere existence. Sure, I was smart and the typical "pre-pharmacy" major, but the crown gave me an outlet to activate rarely used talents, revealing the gifts that I continue to use today. My goal is to provide you a brief look at my reign and how my God-ordained experience as Miss Texas Southern University 2011-2012 prepared me for my purpose as the millennial version of the Proverbs 31:10 woman I am striving to become day by day.

During my reign, I was privileged to mentor a group of 15 freshmen women known as the Miss TSU Crown Jewels, some of which who later became campus queens and even Miss TSU. I wanted to share my experiences as a campus queen as a way to ignite something within them. They traveled and sat with me at football games, graced the stage with me at our "Freshmen Rock the House," participated in service projects throughout the campus, and ultimately, we bonded through weekly personal development seminars. Additionally, I was able to fulfill an element of my platform through a project called Dress a Girl Around the World, a movement to provide beautiful pillowcase dresses to orphans in South Africa. I was privileged to personally deliver them while studying abroad at Stellenbosch University in South Africa the summer after my reign concluded. The entire campus donated decorative pillowcases, transformed the pillowcases into dresses, and donated toward the shipment to South Africa.

I also joined a sisterhood with other campus queens at the Hall of Fame HBCU queen Pageant, winning "Best Overall Queen," an award complimenting my character off the competition stage. Last, but certainly not least, I pledged the most prestigious sisterhood of Delta Sigma Theta Sorority, Incorporated during my reign. There was an insurmountable amount of highs and lows, contributing to developing grit. The exhilarating year was a whirlwind of commitments and exhaustion, but I'd be remiss if I didn't share with you how I converted growing pains into jewels of wisdom that contributed to the woman I am today. Below are a few jewels of wisdom I garnered throughout my journey as a campus queen that were pivotal toward the purpose work I am currently doing as a proud educator, influencer and community organizer.

1. **Carry yourself as if you already have the crown before you win the crown.**

I decided to run for Miss Texas Southern University in the fall of 2009, two years before the pageant in 2011. At the time, I had no clue about pageants, but I wanted the campus to view me as a queen. For two years, I wore my *invisible crown*. I was active in student-centered organizations, dressed in trendy conservative threads, and was respectful toward everyone from the janitor to the president. Additionally, I increased my campus visibility as Miss Sophomore and Miss Black & Gold; both titles were just steppingstones toward the ultimate goal. Moving strategically was key. I was even particular about taking pictures with alcoholic beverages in my hand at campus parties. My intentionality reminds me of the Proverbs 18:22: *A man who findeth a wife findeth a good thing*. Sister girl didn't magically become a wife once she was found. She was already "wifey material" before the man or the engagement ring arrived! The same principle relates today as a professional woman. Allow your counterparts to catch glimpses of your leadership qualities. Although you already know what you are capable of, others have to see it in your actions. So, sis, always wear your invisible crown.

1. Do not allow anyone's definition of a queen to overrule yours.

While preparing for the pageant, I was told numerous times that I needed to install my pageant hair to compete. You know the hair "queens" wear. My peers were adamant and convinced me that wearing a sew-in would help me win the competition by looking more like a "queen." I stood firm by unpopular opinion to remain natural. I knew that if I won, the crown was going to be placed on my little golden natural afro. Hair doesn't validate *queendom*; character and integrity does! I am an advocate for growth; however, it is also important to know who you are at the core and adamantly choose not to waver from your core.

1. Make being uncomfortable the new norm.

There were countless roadblocks I had to overcome to achieve my goal of becoming a campus queen. One roadblock that rocked me to my core was the panel interview. I was literally trembling from the inside out during both panel interviews at a local and national level campus queen competition. The infamous panel interview taught me how to become comfortable with revealing who I am through answering strategic questions. The best piece of advice I received was to be well-read and to always have a quote in your back pocket that aligned with your platform. Years later, I implemented the strategy on a panel interview with district decision-makers when bidding to open a new personalized learning middle school as a co-founder. After successfully interviewing, I called my Miss TSU advisor to thank her for preparing me for my "purpose encounter." All failed experiences serve as a conduit toward mastering a "purpose encounter" in the future.

Ultimately, becoming Miss Texas Southern University 2011-2012 was the most profound experience I could have ever grown through. Therefore, I will continue to use my "reserved seat" at the table to advocate for children who are directly impacted by the decisions made there. My HBCU shaped and cultivated me into the trailblazer who I am today. I am relentless and unapologetic. I am a bridge builder who has been afforded the opportunity to advocate for children with poise and clarity. I am aware that if you're not sitting at the table, you are on the menu. Texas Southern University ignited an endless flame, and I am proud to be a part of a legacy of queens and change agents who boldly left their indelible mark on the infamous Tiger Walk.

About Shartajeye' Wright

Shartajeye' "Taji" Wright is a PROUD graduate of Texas Southern University, serving as the 65th Miss Texas Southern University reigning during the 2011-12 school year. She is considered an “edu-advocate” as a CO-Founder of a personalized learning middle school in Dallas, Texas. Her STEM background enables her to specialize in turnaround innovation, a skill that allows her to work to turn around urban schools through a lens of intentional pedagogy and personalized learning. Her ongoing journey in education has proven that ALL kids, regardless of family structures, language barriers, or prior failures can rise to meet the high expectations set forth. She approaches her craft with authentic passion, content mastery, and compassion for the holistic student.

Outside of the classroom, her fight for equity continues as she serves on the leadership board for Dallas CORE. Dallas CORE is grounded in truth and equity and leverages the power of organized people to create lasting equitable systems in Dallas for all children. She is also the creator of FOREVER31Ruby, a movement empowering the modern-day virtuous woman to reclaim her crown through providing practical advice weekly. Her #dateyouboo mantra echos truth aligned to the virtues of the Proverbs 31 woman (Proverbs 31:10). Taji is motivated by purpose, therefore, her journey will continue to unfold in ways beyond her imagination on a local and global level.

Follow the movement on Instagram @forever31ruby.

STEPHENIE TIDWELL

What A&T Taught Me

Stephenie Tidwell

Miss North Carolina A&T State University 1986-1987

There is no way you are birthed to two people born and raised in the south under Jim Crow segregation, and *not* have the fight for social justice in your blood. More so, there is no way you are born to two Aggies, and they *not* teach you, "Aggie Born, Aggie Bred, and When I Die, I'll be Aggie Dead." My parents raised my brother and me under that mantra. We "walked the yard" annually on our annual vacation pilgrimage, from Passaic, New Jersey and Washington D.C. to Williamston, North Carolina, Greensboro, North Carolina to Kannapolis, North Carolina, finally ending back up in New Jersey. Annually, these trips were history lessons, conversations with their former professors, and stops by family and friends' homes. These were years of training, whether we knew it or not. This was my parents' soul and character-building work. It was years of guidance and preparation for our turn. Then, in August of 1983, Aggieland became my reality.

I will never forget the feeling of being on campus that August, walking the yard and meeting new people at every turn. We walked in droves many times, learning a little history every step of the way and meeting new classmates along the way. Many times, only to discover that our parents were former classmates. Immediate bonds formed as you realized that you were standing on royal ground. Then we met the campus royalty, the SGA President and Ms. A&T. At that point, we realized the significance and tightness of the community we were joining. We realized that being an Aggie was a real blessing.

As a student at such a historical university, we enjoyed all that attending A&T had to offer – the step shows, the homecomings, the concerts and assemblies. But we also joined forces with folks of like mind. We mobilized and joined organizations that had purpose and sought to make a positive change because there was a feeling that just boiled up inside you, letting you know you had a responsibility to those before you. You felt that obligation to use your life to make an impact. Just as my parents talked to us as children about their professors having an impact on their lives, I have to tell you the professors in the Economics Department made an impact on me. Dr. Simmons, Dr. Coley, Dr. Jeong and Dr. Obeng, helped me to understand the world through the lens of an Economist. Then there was Dr. Wayman McLaughlin in the Humanities Department. *What* an impact he made on me, he was the great thinker, who fostered thought and moved you to act.

My professors didn't just teach you your coursework; they talked to you about social unrest, unjust situations, history [your history], and your call to action. I'll never forget Dr. Simmons explaining his father's will to vote and being asked to count how many bubbles in a bar of soap. Their stories served a purpose. Our professors let us know that they had high expectations of us, on the career front, and in the work toward social injustice. So yes, when a small group of the KKK members decided they wanted to march through A&T's campus, we met them face to face. In 1987, when there was civil unrest in Forsyth County, Georgia, as Miss A&T- a member of the Student Government Association, you boarded the bus and went to confront injustice. Serving as Miss A&T meant that you knew your role was not just that of the campus figurehead who was called to speak at university events. I had to do more than represent the university across the city, state, or nation. As Miss A&T, I understood that I was setting an example for others. I was given a platform by the student population to *be* the voice, speak up, and speak out.

Then, one day, campus life comes to an end. You set your sights on representing Aggie greatness and the university in your newfound role of graduate. Quickly, you realize that the lessons from the yard are still with you. You recognize that the experiences you had prepared you well. You continue to be that example as you grow into an adult with lived experiences. You find your passion and the platform that allows you to continue to speak up and speak out. Today, for me, that passion is teaching math. The platform is creating culturally relevant math teachers who are focused on instilling an "identity of achievement" (Delpit, 2012; Ladson-

Billings) as "doers of mathematics" (Aguirre, Mayfield-Ingram & Marin, 2013, p.14). I am committed to fostering teachers who produce students who question societal ills and seek to make changes to our societal landscape.

Life has come full circle. I left Corporate America 19 years ago to join the education field to answer the call of my purpose and my passion. I have become my parents' teachers; I have become *my teachers*. I continue to lead in life as a "communal" educator, one who is anchored in traditional African edifications. I am focused on fostering a collective "identity of achievement and excellence" that is based on teacher belief in and appeal for student intellect, humanity, and spirituality. Today, as a teacher, teacher of teachers, and educational researcher, I look at the picture of how the field of education can create pools of competent math teachers through the lens of understanding that educational research must have a more significant presence in teacher preparation and professional learning.

References

Aguirre, J., Mayfield-Ingram, K., & Martin, D. B. (2013). The impact of identity in K-8

mathematics learning and teaching: Rethinking equity-based practices. Va: NCTM.

Delpit, Lisa. D. (2012). *"Multiplication is for white people": Raising expectations for other*

people's children. New York: New Press: Distributed by Perseus Distribution.

Ladson-Billings, G. (1994/2009). *The dreamkeepers: Successful teachers of African American*

children. San Francisco: Jossey-Bass Publishers.

About Stephenie Tidwell

Education is Stephenie's second career and her first love. Stephenie spent 16 years in the Banking and Finance Industry before leaving in 2001 to become a Math Teacher. When asked, "If you were not in the field of banking what would you do?" She always responded, "Teach math". She has worked as a Supervisor of Mathematics in several New Jersey Districts, supervising as many as 150 educational professionals at times. In her position she has initiated professional learning communities to support teacher development and enhance student achievement, implemented the use of common formative assessments, introduced educational technology to support student comprehension and engagement, created a professional development website, and established partnerships with out-of-district schools to promote peer observations and collaboration. Her signature accomplishment was an In-District Math Teacher Institute. This four-phase institute included a series of summer workshops to address the mathematics knowledge required for elementary teachers to effectively implement the Common Core Standards, school-year in-class coaching and debriefing sessions to address teacher practice and implementation of the standards, and in-district college course offerings during the school year. She credits these opportunities with enhancing her organizational and leadership skills while creating a culture of collaboration centered on student achievement.

Stephenie's strength in data analysis, budget development, curriculum development, action plan development, workshop development and seminar presentation, and staff evaluation have assisted her in being an effective educational leader and resource for her staff. She maintains that an education leader is an effective instructional leader that encourages collegiality for the sake of promoting open and honest discussions about teaching practices and instruction; moving teachers beyond coverers of materials towards educational intellects focused creating equitable and socially just experiences for students.

Stephenie holds a Degree in Economics from North Carolina Agricultural and Technical State University and two a Masters's Degree from Montclair State University (MA Social Science with a concentration in Economics and MA Educational Leadership). She is a 2022 Doctoral candidate in Teacher Education and Teacher Development. She holds NJ certifications for the positions of: School Administrator, Principal, Supervisor, Mathematics, and Elementary Education K-8.

Stephenie is currently employed by the Princeton Board of Education where she serves as the District Supervisor of Mathematics and Business Education. She continues to increase her knowledge and skills by reading current literature, participating in professional development activities, and maintaining memberships in professional organizations. She resides in Union, NJ with her son Joshua Tidwell.

JORDAN WATKINS

The Courage to Walk in the Right Direction

Jordan Watkins

Miss Lawson State College 2016-2017

When I was asked to talk about my experience as an HBCU queen, I was delighted. I wanted to share my experience, give hope and relate to others. As soon as the excitement settled, I started to become fearful. *What I would say? What if what I have to say isn't good enough? What if it doesn't help anyone?* I researched different HBCU queens. I reviewed my outgoing speak and tried to reminisce on the times during my reign. Although all of these things had a positive impact, they really didn't help me feel any more secure in my brainstorming process. I was going to have to dig a little deeper and ask myself why I wanted to contribute to this book, why I cherish my HBCU, and who I want to thank.

As I pondered these questions, I remembered the courage and the lessons the people from Lawson have continued to give me. I want to share that courage with as many people as possible. In the words of Mary Anne Radmacher, "Courage doesn't always roar. Sometimes courage is the little voice at the end of the day that says, 'I'll try again tomorrow.'" In other words, working hard for what you want is about the progression that is made from day to day and the courage to start walking in the right direction.

I started my walk when I enrolled at Lawson State Community College straight out of high school. I had no idea where I was going or how I was going to get there. My only goal was to go to class and go home. I was way out of my comfort zone. I didn't want to draw attention to myself since I really didn't plan on making any friends. In an attempt to hide myself so I wouldn't be found, Beatrice Collins, a previous Miss Lawson State queen reached out to me. She advised me to become a Lawson State Ambassador. After our conversation, I figured I didn't have anything to lose.

Shortly after joining the ambassadors, I met one of my best friends, Karl Anthony Pruitt, II. Karl and I shortly bonded over our love for helping others, making a difference and sharing our experiences. In order to grasp a greater understanding of my impact, I called Karl and asked him, "What should I say?"

He told me, "Be honest and share your heart."

After a conversation that led to a couple of heartwarming tears, I came face-to-face with the fear of failing to continue offering sincere acts of service to those I lead. I cried over the thought of not being able to provide comfort to those who have felt overlooked, underrepresented or underserved.

Truth is, I have felt *all* of those emotions.

Nevertheless, shortly after a year of being at Lawson State Community College, I was not only a member of the choir, but the honors college and Kappa Beta Delta. I was also an executive member of the Student Government Association and Phi Beta Lambda. These roles taught me valuable lessons, such as preparation, leadership, persistence and patience. I was given the task to delegate duties to officers, draw out a timeline of successes and failures, and provide student feedback to faculty members. Because of my active participation, I was asked to run for Miss Lawson State. I was extremely nervous. But from the support of mentors I had gained, I accepted the challenge. Becoming Miss Lawson State was such a rewarding moment. I remember Mr. D, a faculty member, approaching me the day after I was crowned.

He asked, "Do you finally feel accomplished?"

Shocked, I don't remember if I even responded. But all I remember thinking was, *I haven't done anything yet.*

Once I was crowned, I had entered a world of responsibility. I was asked to speak on behalf of the institution at formal functions, participate in community service, manage available time in my schedule to make appearances at the request of the President, provide student feedback and hold a standard of excellence in the classroom. At this point, I was no longer Jordan Watkins. I was a representation of the student body who considered me to play the role of an accessible sister, confidant and mentor, while also doubling as a student recruiter and broadcasting the success stories of the institution. I not only wanted to play the role, but I wanted to live in it daily. In the words of Michael S. Miller, "People don't care how much you know until they know how much you care."

In the midst of higher expectations being placed upon me, there was an added sense of consciousness to everything I did. A consciousness to continue to provide wholeness, healing and opportunities to those who needed it most. We've all heard the quote, "Hurt people hurt people." Alternatively, "Healing people heal people." I saw this role as an opportunity to speak to those who have been ignored, respect those who had been disrespected, and honor those who didn't feel honorable. I wanted to enhance the law of addition, which states that the best way to add value is by serving others, seeking always to do some good somewhere, and assisting others in becoming the person they were meant to be.

The desire I possessed to add value pushed me—not only to be a student leader—but to be a mature leader who first listened, learned, then led. I listened to how students communicated, how they talked to each other and about each other. I knew I had to do better. In my request to do better, I actively searched for opportunities to enhance my character by exemplifying authentic acts of service. As I continued to do this, I found myself spending more time with students, learning new things and hearing their stories. Stories of domestic abuse, failure and shame were shared as a result of a broken community who has failed those who lived in it.

My personal mission as Miss Lawson State was to enhance the community in which the students lived. I also wanted to participate in projects that would actively represent the student body and the voices of those who had been suffering in silence. I worked tediously, with the help of faculty and friends, to enhance the community by healing hearts, volunteering, broadening perspectives and listening to those who had something to say. Some days, I came to Lawson as early as, or earlier than, 8 a.m. and left around 10 p.m. to plan projects, offer rides homes or tutor students. Throughout the community, I partnered with Habitat for

Humanity, offered my services to local churches, educated myself on homelessness, volunteered with high school students, and expanded my reach by attending leadership conferences. I wanted to ensure that I offered my best self in every situation. Additionally, I worked with faculty to propose ideas for scholarships, committees and programs that would enhance the experiences of each student.

The opportunity that I was presented with to continuously serve others has reminded me to be the change that I want to see in the world. From this experience that I will cherish forever, I constantly work to help others through advocation, education or motivation. Today, after graduating from Lawson State with an Associate in Business Administration, serving on the homecoming court at the University of Alabama, then graduating with a Bachelor of Accounting, working on my Master of Higher Education Administration, and pursuing my entrepreneurial endeavors with my partnership in Beautycounter, I have continued to live by the motto of: "Leave any situation better than I found it." In response to Mr. D, yes, I finally feel accomplished. But there is still work to be done, and I don't plan on stopping anytime soon.

About Jordan Watkins

My name is Jordan Watkins. I graduated from Lawson State Community College in 2017 with an Associates Degree in Business Administration. After graduating from Lawson State, I transferred to the University of Alabama. In the summer of 2019 I graduated from the University of Alabama with a Bachelors in Accounting. I have continued my education by pursuing a Masters in Higher Education Administration with the hopes of focusing on education psychology. I want to share my story in hopes of inspiring others to be authentic in their leadership and in helping those around them enhance their true potential in life. Currently as a Beautycounter consultant I have been able to educate women on the importance of health and wellness and self care. I have been blessed with the opportunity to make an impact center around personal development that pays. I plan to continue to inspire women as a motivational speaker as I partner with local business, social workers, and influencers to focus on mental health, financial freedom, and inclusiveness. Additionally, I want to start a girls organization that focuses on supporting young women, enhancing their potential and maximizing their strengths.

IASHEA LAKENYA SIMMONS

I Dream In Color

Iashea Lakenya Simmons

Miss Morris College 2006-2007

When I was a young girl filled with so much innocence, ambition and eagerness, I didn't have any role models. I didn't have anyone encouraging me to reach my full potential. What I do remember is my single-parent mother teaching me to be independent, spending endless hours in our backyard teaching me how to ride my bicycle (and how excited she was when I finally got it). She worked beside me on a D.A.R.E. project, for which I won first place. My mom has always been such a hard-working woman. She encouraged my sister and I to become a teacher or a nurse, apparently not realizing that we needed to attend college to achieve either. To be honest, I was not informed about college being an option for me until my senior year of high school. By then, I had no plans to attend.

It Takes a Village

I pay homage to those who helped mold me throughout my young adult life and aided with preparing me for my college journey. It truly takes a village.

In 1997, while attending Cainhoy Junior-Senior High School, I met Alisha Mitchell and her entire Mitchell-Washington Family. We quickly became friends. Alisha soon invited me to her house to spend the weekend with her family. As months went on, our weekends became filled with adventurous moments, such as early Saturday morning yard sales, Young People Division activities, and church on Sunday. During the summer months, we spent our time with Alisha's aunt and Uncle Jeff, Debra and their young daughters in Pinewood, South Carolina (Sumter County). Amid all the fun weekends and exciting summers, Alisha's family inspired her to prepare to attend Morris College.

I missed the school bus one afternoon of my senior year. While walking home, it seemed like the longest walk of my life. However, in that moment,

I realized I was lost and filled with so much uncertainty. I was covered by what seemed to be a generational curse. Those before me could only give me the best they had been given. In 2002, I graduated high school and started working one dead-end job after another, living from paycheck to paycheck. I knew I wanted so much more, but I was either unsure of how to obtain it, or I was afraid to reach for it.

My Changing Moment

At the age of twenty-one, I finally realized that I had to take control of my own destiny. So, with not much prior planning, I enrolled at Morris College. I was literally accepted to the college on the day my mother and older brother drove me on campus for freshman orientation. The biggest impact on my life the day I arrived on the campus of Morris College was meeting Mrs. Deborah Calhoun, Director of Admissions and Records. She spoke life into my future success by believing in me when I could not see clearly throughout a confusing day.

Mrs. Calhoun's statement to me, which I will never forget, was, "You are going to do well here. I can see it in you. I believe in you."

During the first semester of my freshman year, I felt I was just blowing in the wind. I was just trying to figure things out and see where I fit in, while doing my best to remain focused. As the spring semester approached an end, I kept Mrs. Calhoun's words close to my heart. I pushed harder and decided to enroll in the summer school sessions.

As the semesters came and passed, I became more active on campus and in the community. I realized that I wanted to reach young children just like me, those who had not been given the proper tools to ignite their inner potential. The North Hope Center and The Greenhouse Runaway Shelter were the steppingstones to me being able to be of service to those in my community. While working at these places, I discovered a flame was ignited within my soul, a flame that told me to, "Meet one, teach one!" I tried to breathe life into each child and/or young person in need who I encountered.

My Reign as Miss Morris College 2006-2007

In February 2006, a seed was planted in me by my advisors, Marguerite Wilder and Sonya Davis Levy, to run for the title of Miss Morris College. They both warned me that it would be a tremendous responsibility. But through their encouragement, they convinced me that I was up to the challenge. After weeks of campaigning, dormitory visits, campus debates and numerous acts of service, it was time for the student body to cast their votes. The night the votes were being tallied seemed like the longest night of my life. I tossed and turned and paced my dorm room from corner to corner. The next day, Dean Sanford called me into her office and gave me the wonderful news that I was elected by the student body to represent Morris College as the 2006-2007 campus Queen. I could barely contain my excitement!

The night of my coronation in October 2006 was the most memorable and humbling experience of my life to that point. Being crowned Miss Morris College was groundbreaking for me. It was the moment I knew the real work was just beginning. I realized everything that had been embedded into my soul by my village had molded me to pay it forward and pass it on to others in need. I began speaking with youths in safe havens, shelters and other juveniles, encouraging them to dream and never give up until their dreams become reality.

We all have a divine purpose on this journey called life. We must acknowledge our purpose and press forward to overcome any obstacles.

My Platform

Being Miss Morris College has molded me into a motivational warrior, a mentor for the youth, an amazing mother, and a safe haven for children who need to be encouraged to reach their full potential. I have and I am continuing to utilize the platform of a Queen to encourage and cheer on others through their rough patches in life. My inner love for humanity and service has awarded me the opportunity to travel, serving on missions' trips to Cape Town, South Africa, Egpyt, Marrakesh and Casablanca, Morocco.

Life Quotes

"If your actions create a legacy that inspire others to dream more, learn more, do more and become more, then you are an excellent leader."

Dolly Parton

Special Thanks

To my lovely family: my mother, Florence R. Ford; my delightful grandparents, Mr. and Mrs. Clarence Simmons; The Drayton Family; The Mitchell-Washington Family; The Dingle Family; Ms. Yvonne Firby; The Spann Family; Vivia Gamble; David "Reb" Lewis; Mrs. Deborah Calhoun; The Dupree Family; The Jenkins Family; The Barnwell Family; Dr. Adeleri Onisegun; Dr. L. Green; Ms. Sonya Davis Levy; Ms. Marguerite Wilder; and Ms. Linda Richbow.

About Iashea Lakenya Simmons

Iashea Lakenya Simmons is married to Thomas Dashiell. On August 15, 2019 she became a new and proud mom to Tommie Eli.

Iashea was born and raised in beautiful, sunny Charleston, SC. Shortly after graduating Wando High School she attended and graduated from Morris College in Sumter, SC majoring in Criminal Justice with a concentration in Psychology. In the Fall of 2004 Iashea became a member of Zeta Phi Beta Sorority Inc. at Morris College and served as President of the Pi Theta Chapter.

Iashea was elected by her peers to serve as Miss Morris College 2006-2007. During her reign, she worked diligently on and off campus with the following organizations and agencies to encourage adolescent and adult development and physical activity: The Greenhouse Runaway shelter; South Hope Resource Center after school program; Probation, Parole & Pardon Services.

Iashea's personal journey since college, in her words, is described below:

"After graduation my mother and I packed my car along with a 16-passenger van with what little belongings I owned (a full size bed, a wooden bookshelf given to me by my grandparents… which I still have to this very day, a TV so small I couldn't read the captions with a magnifying glass.. lol) and I moved to Charlotte, NC to begin working in my field of study. I worked for the Mecklenburg County Child Support Enforcement and Judiciary system for 11 years. Suddenly, I had the desire to learn more about the human anatomy and how it all worked together. I resigned my position and enrolled at Carolinas College of Health Science, where I earned my Surgical Technology degree. After graduating I worked at Carolinas Medical Center on the Trauma Teams gaining level 1 experience working at the operative site scrubbing Neurology, General, Pediatrics, Orthopedic, and Urology cases.

After spending a year on the trauma team, I was ready to learn so much more and specialize in a specific service line. My cousin recommended applying with the VA under the recent graduate program. I wanted to make momentous changes, so I applied and within weeks I accepted a job with the George E. Wahlen VA Medical Center in Salt Lake City, Utah. I became the service line tech for the Vascular and Robotic surgical teams, scrubbing Open Abdominal Aortic Aneurysm, Endovascular Repair of Abdominal Aortic Aneurysm, Robotic Prostatectomy and Robotic Nissen procedures. What an amazing adventure and life-changing experience that was!

I eventually decided that I was ready to return home, so during the past year I relocated back to Charleston to be closer to family. I am currently employed at the local VA Hospital, still helping others and doing the work I love."

What do you do for fun?

Iashea is extremely adventurous! She has traveled to 48 of the 50 states, and 5 of the 7 continents. ("I'm willing to try anything once" she says.. #YOLO). She loves traveling, hiking, and learning about other cultures. Her favorite thing: Spending time with family and girlfriends for fun.

(Pictured below: Iashea visiting Robben Island Museum in South Africa)

Official Partners & Sponsors of The HBCU Experience Movement, LLC

Baker & Baker Realty, LLC

Christopher Baker- CEO/Founder
Instagram: seedougieblake
Facebook: Christopher D. Baker
Email: baker.christopher@gmail.com

Bound By Conscious Concepts

Kathryn Lomax-CEO/Founder
Instagram: msklovibes223
Facebook: Klo-Kathryn Lomax
Contact: (972) 638-9823
Email: Klomax@bbconcepts.com

Dancer NC Dance District

Dr. Kellye Worth Hall
Instagram: divadoc5
Facebook: Kellye Worth Hall
Email: delta906@gmail.com

HBCU Wall Street

Torrence Reed & Jamerus Peyton-CEO/Founders
Facebook: HBCU Wall Street
Email: info@hbcuwallstreet.com

Springbreak Watches (SPGBK)

Kwame Molden- CEO/Founder
Instagram: SPGBK
Facebook: Kwame Molden
Email: info@springbreakwatches.com

Minority Cannabis Business Association

Shanita Penny- President
Instagram- Minority Cannabis
Facebook- MCBA.Org
Twitter- MinCannBusAssoc
LinkedIn- Minority Cannabis Business Association
Email-info@minoritycannabis.org
Website: www.MinorityCannabis.org
Phone: 202-681-2889

The Phoenix Professional Network

DJavon Alston-Owner/Founder
Instagram: thephoenixnetwork757
Facebook: DJavon Alston
Email: thephoenixnetwork757@gmail.com

Never2Fly2Pray

Jeffrey Lee Sawyer: Owner/Founder
Instagram: never2fly2pray
Facebook: Jeffrey Lee
Email htdogwtr@yahoo.com

Allen Financial Solutions

Jay Allen: Owner/Founder
Instagram: jay83allen
Facebook: Jay Allen
Email: allen.jonathan83@gmail.com

Holistic Practitioners

Tianna Bynum: CEO/Founder
Facebook: Tianna Bynum
Email tpb33@georgetown.edu

Journee Enterprises

Fred Whit: CEO/Founder
Facebook: Fred Whit
Instagram: frederickwjr
Email: frederickwjr@yahoo.com

Company: Ashley Little Enterprises, LLC

Ashley Little- CEO/Founder
Facebook: Ashley Little
Instagram: _ashleyalittle
Email: aalittle08@gmail.com

HBCU Pride Nation

CEO/ Founder: Travis Jackson
Instagram: hbcupridenation
Facebook: HBCU Pride Nation
Email: travispjackson@gmail.com

LK Productions

CEO/Founder: Larry King
Instagram: lk_rrproduction
Facebook: Larry King
Email: lk_production@yahoo.com

NXLEVEL TRAVEL (NXLTRVL)

Chief Executive Officer Hercules Conway
Chief Operating Officer Newton Dennis
Instagram-nxlevel
Instagram: herc3k
Facebook-Newton Dennis
Facebook: Hercules Conway
Email Address: info@nxleveltravel.com
Website: NXLEVELTRAVEL.COM

BLKWOMENHUSTLE

CEO/Founder: Lashawn Dreher
Instagram: blkwomenhustle
Facebook: Blk Women Hustle
Email: info@blkwomenhustle.com

HBCU Grad
CEO/Founder Todd Finley
www.hbcugraduates.com
312-535-8511

Campaign
Engineers

Campaign Engineers

Chris Smith, CEO/Founder
Instagram: csmithatl
Email Address: csmith1911@gmail.com

Boardroom Brand LLC

Samuel Brown III, CEO/Founder
Instagram:_gxxdy
Email Address: samuel.brown.three@gmail.com

HBCU 1010

Jahliel Thurman, CEO/Founder
www.hbcu101.com
Instagram: hbcu101
jahlielthurman@gmail.com

Uplift Clothing Apparel

Jermaine Simpson, CEO/Founder
UpliftClothingApparel.com
Instagram: Upliftclothingapparel

AC Events The Luxury Planning Experience

Amy Agbottah, CEO/Founder:
Email Address: amy@amycynthiaevents.com

PIXRUS Photo Booth

Natan Mckenzie, CEO/Founder
Email Address: Natan.mckenzie@gmail.com
Instagram: pixrusghana

MMInvestments

Tarik McAllister, CEO/Founder:
Instagram: MMInvestments
Email Address: tarik@mmibuilders.com

AllThingsLoop

Kenya Nalls, CEO/Founder:
Email Address: staff@allthingsloop.com
Contact Number: 773-939-0680

Historically Black Since

CEO/Founder: Adrena Martin
Instagram: historicallyblacksince
www.hbcusince.com

February First

CEO/Founder: Cedric Livingston
www.februaryfirstmovie.com
Director/Writer February First: A Stride Towards Freedom

HBCU Times

David Staten, Ph.
hbcutimes@gmail.com
Facebook: HBCU Times
Instagram: hbcu_times8892
Bridget Hollis Staten, Ph.D

Swing Into Their Dreams Foundation

Pamela Parker and Lynn Demmons, Co-Founders
Email Address: swingintotheirdreams@gmail.com
Website: swingintotheirdreams.com

Harbor Institute

CEO/Founder: Rasheed Ali Cromwell, JD
Instagram: @theharborinstitute
Facebook: The Harbor Institute
Twitter: @harborinstitute
Email: racromwell@theharborinstitute.com

HBCU Pulse

CEO/Founder Randall Barnes
Website: hbcupulse.com
Instagram: @hbcupulse
Twitter: @thehbcupulse

SwagHer

Vice President Of Sales/Marketing Jarmel Roberson
Website www.swagher.net
instagram: swaghermagazine
Email Address: jroberson@swagher.net

H.E.R. Story Podcast

Janea Jamison|Creator
H.E.R. Story with J. Jamison
#Herstorymovement
IG : @herstory_podcast

HBCU Buzz

LUKE LAWAL JR.
lawal@lcompany.co
Fndr, CEO | (301) 221-1719 @lukelawal
L & COMPANY { *HBCU Buzz* | *Taper, Inc.* | *Root Care Health* }

Zoom Technologies, LLC

Torrence Reed - CEO/Founder
Instagram: torrencereed3
Email: support@zoom-technologies.co

Yard Talk 101

Jahliel Thurman CEO/Founder
Instagram: YardTalk101
Website: YardTalk101.com

Chef Batts

Keith Batts-CEO/Founder
Instagram: chefbatts
Email: booking@chefbatts.com

Johnson Capital

Marcus Johnson CEO/Founder
Instagram: marcusdiontej
Email: marcus@johnsoncap.com

SheIsMagazine
CEO/Founder: Ciara Horton
Instagram:@sheisemagazine
Facebook:Ciara Horton
Email: ciarasheisemagazine.com

Success and Religion
CEO/Founder: Micheal Taylor
Email: Successismyreligion@gmail.com

Queen Series
CEO/Founder: Randall Barnes
Email: aqueenseries@gmail.com

HBCU Girls Talk
CEO/Founder: TeeCee Camper
Instagram: @hbcugirlstalk
Contact: talkgirls@yahoo.com

www.ingramcontent.com/pod-product-compliance
Lightning Source LLC
LaVergne TN
LVHW012333100826
845148LV00017B/2279
* 9 7 8 1 7 3 4 9 3 1 1 2 9 *